THE INSIDER'S GUIDE TO
MAKING MONEY IN
REAL ESTATE

D0196333

THE INSIDER'S GUIDE TO
MAKING MONEY IN
REAL ESTATE

Smart Steps to Building
Your Wealth Through Property

Dolf de Roos, PhD
Diane Kennedy, CPA

WILEY

John Wiley & Sons, Inc.

Copyright © 2005 by Dolf de Roos and Diane Kennedy. All rights reserved.

Published by John Wiley & Sons, Inc., Hoboken, New Jersey.
Published simultaneously in Canada.

No part of this publication may be reproduced, stored in a retrieval system, or transmitted in any form or by any means, electronic, mechanical, photocopying, recording, scanning, or otherwise, except as permitted under Section 107 or 108 of the 1976 United States Copyright Act, without either the prior written permission of the Publisher, or authorization through payment of the appropriate per-copy fee to the Copyright Clearance Center, Inc., 222 Rosewood Drive, Danvers, MA 01923, (978) 750-8400, fax (978) 646-8600, or on the web at www.copyright.com. Requests to the Publisher for permission should be addressed to the Permissions Department, John Wiley & Sons, Inc., 111 River Street, Hoboken, NJ 07030, (201) 748-6011, fax (201) 748-6008.

Limit of Liability/Disclaimer of Warranty: While the publisher and author have used their best efforts in preparing this book, they make no representations or warranties with respect to the accuracy or completeness of the contents of this book and specifically disclaim any implied warranties of merchantability or fitness for a particular purpose. No warranty may be created or extended by sales representatives or written sales materials. **The publisher is not engaged in rendering professional services. The advice and strategies contained herein may not be suitable for your situation and the reader should seek professional advice with respect to specific situations that may arise.** Neither the publisher nor author shall be liable for any loss of profit or any other commercial damages, including but not limited to special, incidental, consequential, or other damages.

For general information on our other products and services, or technical support, please contact our Customer Care Department within the United States at 800-762-2974, outside the United States at 317-572-3993 or fax 317-572-4002.

Wiley also publishes its books in a variety of electronic formats. Some content that appears in print may not be available in electronic books. For more information about Wiley products, visit our web site at www.wiley.com.

Designations used by companies to distinguish their products are often claimed by trademarks. In all instances where the author or publisher is aware of a claim, the product names appear in Initial Capital letters. Readers, however, should contact the appropriate companies for more complete information regarding trademarks and registration.

Library of Congress Cataloging-in-Publication Data:

De Roos, Dolf.
    The insider's guide to making money in real estate : smart steps to building your wealth through prosperity / Dolf de Roos and Diane Kennedy.
        p.   cm.
    Includes index.
    ISBN 0-471-71177-2 (pbk.)
    1. Real estate investment.   2. Investments.   I. Kennedy, Diane, 1956–   II. Title.
HD1382.5.D468   2004
332.63'24—dc22   2004062833

Printed in the United States of America.

10 9 8 7 6 5 4 3 2 1

Acknowledgments

The authors would like to acknowledge the following people for their help with this book:

Beverly Adams, John Baen, Claudia Brelo, James Burgin, Ken Burlington, Richard Cooley, Sherri Cossman, Catrina Craft, Amy Fox, Michael Hamilton, Elaine Harshbarger, Laurie Harting, Megan Hughes, Larry Jellen, Gina Jerome, Mingoo Kang, Cindy Kenney, Robert McCoy, Gabe Mendoza, Scott Mertens, Morgan Smith, Chris Szabo, Alex Tanner, Pamela Williams, and Paul Wolf.

It wouldn't have been possible without each one of you!

The 1 million members of the NATIONAL ASSOCIATION OF REALTORS® (NAR) are dedicated to assisting families in achieving the American dream of home ownership. Only real estate professionals who are members of NAR may call themselves REALTORS®. All REALTORS® must subscribe to NAR's strict Code of Ethics, which is based on honesty, professionalism and the protection of the public. Consult a REALTOR® in your area today or log onto www.Realtor.com to find a REALTOR® to help you buy or sell a home.

Contents

CONTENTS

Introduction

Do you dislike your job, distrust your boss, dread each day, and fear you might lose the job you can't stand? Well, if you do, then you're like millions of other Americans today who want the freedom that more money would bring. However, unless you're willing to take massive action today, in 10 years' time you will still dislike your job, distrust your boss, dread each day, and fear you might lose the job you can't stand, with the only difference being that you'll be 10 years older and still longing to be rich, but with 10 years of living gone forever.

Everyone wants to be rich, but few people know exactly what that means. If you cannot create a mental picture of what being rich means for you, how will you ever achieve it? Let's create that image together.

Imagine being awakened by the sun (no ear-splitting alarm clock for you). Your leisurely breakfast is interrupted by a call from a real estate agent asking if you want to sell one of the buildings you bought the previous year for a profit of $150,000. As you gaze out over the ocean, sipping your freshly squeezed orange juice, you weigh the relative merits of selling and decide, in this instance, to keep the building. Your breakfast was interrupted and you still have more decisions to make today, such as whether to go snorkeling or surfing and where to have dinner tonight. But with this one business decision, your working day is over.

Are you ready to put in the effort to go from where you are

now to this idyllic scenario? You can make these dreams come true with real estate. There's work involved, to be sure—some of it will be physical, but most of it will be mental.

As you read through *The Insider's Guide to Making Money in Real Estate*, you might find ideas that challenge what you believe about real estate. Those are the types of ideas that can make huge differences in your life. Remember that this is an "insider's guide." Unlike the stock market, where insider trading can land you huge fines or even jail time, real estate insider information is not only legal, it's also a critical part of creating wealth. Insider information also implies that there will be strategies that are different from what you might have heard through others. Rather than opinions or guesses, you'll learn the actual facts from successful real estate investors who have had years of experience in the market.

HE SAID, SHE SAID

Have you and a friend ever had completely different reasons why you should do something and yet came to exactly the same conclusion? If two different patterns of logic give you same the answer, that gives you a more confident feeling that the conclusion must be right.

Well, that's what has happened for the authors of this book, Dolf de Roos, author of the best-selling *Real Estate Riches—How to Become Rich Using Your Banker's Money*, and Diane Kennedy, author of the best-selling *Loopholes of the Rich—How the Rich Legally Make More Money and Pay Less Tax*. Dolf has always promoted real estate as not just a little better than other forms of building wealth, but actually orders of magnitude better. Diane, a CPA to some of the nation's most wealthy people, looks to real estate for the tremendous tax benefits. In other words, he said, "More income!" and she said, "Less tax!" and they both said "Real estate!"

DOES THIS STUFF REALLY WORK?

Is it really possible to make money investing in real estate? This is an easy question for us to answer. We, the authors of this book, have both been active investors for over 20 years. In fact, we added it up and found that together we have 50 years of experience in real estate (and we looked at each other thinking "That makes *you* quite old!"). And, even more important, despite our active schedules due to our respective businesses and speaking calendars, we are both still prolific real estate investors.

Dolf was offered a job at $32,000 per year when he graduated with his Ph.D. in engineering. His classmates would have been delighted with that offer. But, Dolf had a decision to make. You see, he had also closed on a property that made him $35,000 just the week before he was offered the job. What choice would you have made—making $32,000 per year, working 50 weeks per year, showing up willing and eager to do your boss's bidding, day after day after day, or making $35,000 after one week's activities? Of course if you did not take the job, you would still have to decide what to do with the rest of the year. You might decide to work one more week hoping to repeat your success, or maybe you'll just wonder what to have for lunch and whether you're going swimming in the morning or the afternoon. For Dolf, the decision was easy. Dolf spends time doing what he loves and a large part of what he loves is real estate deals.

Diane's discovery of the merits of real estate investing was a little tougher. She started out working for someone else in the typical 10-hour-day, six-days-a-week cycle. Then, one day she woke up to discover that she had been working really hard, and so far all she had to show for it was (1) a highly paid position in a business that was facing massive layoffs, (2) more debt than assets, and (3) court-ordered alimony payments to an ex-husband. The solution for Diane was to do what her rich clients had always done—start a business and buy real estate. Within five years, she had created enough passive income from real estate to retire. She started a new business again about a year later, but this time she was able to design it to attract the businesses and clients that she wanted to work with. The freedom to pursue her passion is made possible because she invests in real estate to create passive income with huge tax benefits.

But, those are just our stories. Here are a couple more stories of how our clients and customers have been able to use insider's tips to make money in real estate.

PROFESSIONAL ATHLETE STARTS MAKING REAL MONEY

One of Dolf's colleagues is a highly compensated professional ballplayer. One of the problems professional athletes face is that they generally have a very limited career. Once the fans have gone home, what then? Dolf's colleague decided that he didn't want that to happen! So, he teamed up with his brother-in-law to study different markets across the United States. They were looking for appreciating markets in areas they would enjoy visiting and working in. Based on their criteria, they determined that Florida had the best potential. They rec-

4

ognized that there was a lot of money to be made in various ways in real estate. For example, they could make money buying, rehabbing, and selling property. But they wanted to do something that Dolf calls "property with a twist." In other words, they searched for extraordinary profit-making opportunities. They found that they could buy certain properties on a block and then control a large portion of that block. In this way, they leveraged their position to a large developer. Recently they spent nearly $3 million by slowly buying individual properties, and then resold them as a project for over $9 million. They've made a lot of money, and they've also had a significant role in transforming neighborhoods.

NURSE QUITS HER JOB SO SHE CAN MAKE SOME REAL MONEY

Sometimes work gets in the way of making money. That was the case for two clients of Diane's CPA firm. We'll call them Marvin and Joan for purposes of this story. Marvin was a highly compensated doctor and his wife Joan continued to work part-time as a nurse. She did it more for something to do than for the money. Marvin earned a very high income, but he felt trapped. The money they made went to support their high lifestyle. They didn't want to change their lifestyle, but instead looked for ways that they could make more money.

That's why they came to consult with Diane's company. They realized that their single biggest expense was their taxes. Reducing the amount of taxes they paid would be the fastest way they knew to save money. They had also begun buying a few real estate properties that created a little cash flow, but few tax benefits. They lost most of the tax benefits because their income was too high. Taxpayers making over $150,000 per year cannot deduct their real estate passive losses against other income.

Joan was very interested in the real estate. They had invested in an area with a large Spanish-speaking population and she had started Spanish lessons so that she could communicate better with the contractors, property managers, and tenants.

In order to increase their net income, Joan had to quit her job! Joan loved that idea and quickly quit her part-time position as a nurse. She now could easily qualify as a *real estate professional* under the IRS guidelines. As a real estate professional, she and her husband could now take 100 percent of the real estate losses against his income. While becoming a licensed real estate agent involves a considerable investment of time and effort, to qualify as a real estate professional under the IRS guidelines is simply achieved by any of the following three methods.

1. Be employed by a business engaged in a real estate activity (you must own 5 percent or more of the company), or
2. If employed outside of the real estate profession, then more hours must be spent in real estate activities than the other activity in the year (a minimum of 750 hours is required), or
3. If not employed, spend 750 hours per year in real estate activities.

Joan qualified under (3) above. They immediately began taking advantage of the tax benefits from their real estate. With her newfound focus on real estate, Joan began buying more "fix-up" apartment projects, which she then quickly rented. In less than five years, Marvin and Joan made more money from their real estate than they did from Marvin's medical practice. They were financially free and they paid less tax.

HIS BUSINESS IS MOVING

You might have heard the story of Kurt before. He's also a client of Diane's CPA firm, only for years he didn't even file a tax return. Kurt took advantage of special tax laws that apply only to homeowners. He started out by moving into a house in a rapidly improving neighborhood. Not only was this the worst house in the neighborhood, it very well might have been one of the worst houses in all of Phoenix! But, Kurt didn't let that discourage him. He did the fix-up work himself. He had the time to do it as he'd left his job as a banker the month before (after making sure he had a line of credit in place to do the fix-up work needed.) At younger than 30 years old, Kurt no longer needed to work for someone else because he sold that first house for a gain of $110,000 two years later. And he paid no tax because he had lived in the home as his principal residence for two years before he sold the property.

Kurt never needed to work again because he had discovered how just one home loophole could provide a way to create tax-free income.

It's been over seven years since Kurt sold that first property, and he's on his third home now. But, the problem with retiring so young is that sometimes you get bored. So, Kurt bought a historic building in a small city called Miami, Arizona, an hour and a half away from Phoenix. He has started an antiques store there with a partner. Kurt works at the store on weekends, and his business partner takes care of it the rest of the time, while Kurt travels around the United States collecting antiques. For Kurt, it's still all just a vacation, because he's doing what he really loves. Real estate investing through his own house made that possible.

IT REALLY IS WHO YOU KNOW THAT COUNTS

The people around you influence you every day. If they tell you that real estate investing isn't smart, or that the time for good deals is past, or that it's impossible to really do the things you read about in books, then you, at some level, will believe those things. On the other hand, being around positive people will encourage you.

One of the things that Dolf and Diane both do in their businesses is teach the people they work with. And, we've found that no matter where you are, or what your circumstances, it is possible to make money in real estate. We're fortunate to work with Beverly and Amy on a daily basis. Here are their real estate stories.

Beverly is a single mother who has raised her now 17-year-old son completely by herself. She has received no outside help or child support payments and yet, through her hard work, was finally able to save up the down payment for a house. She then wanted to start investing in real estate, but had absolutely no money available. However, Beverly had a highly valuable skill—she was an experienced bookkeeper. She traded that experience and work for part ownership of a real estate partnership. She's now a substantial real estate investor.

Amy acquired her first rental property shortly after her thirtieth birthday. She moved out of the town house she owned into a home in the historic district. She rented out the town house for a positive cash flow of over $300 per month. Her new home has a guest house that she can rent if she wants. For now, though, she enjoys keeping the guest house complete with pool for her out-of-town guests. She also likes having an extra $300 per month.

HOW TO GET MORE OUT OF THIS BOOK

At the end of each chapter, you will find *Action Steps*. The Chinese have a saying:

> I hear and I forget,
> I see and I remember,
> I do and I understand.

If you truly want to change where you are, take the time to do the action steps at the end of each chapter. These steps are designed to move you forward regardless of whether you currently invest in real estate or have not yet invested.

IS IT TOO LATE TO GET STARTED?

We leave this chapter with a true story by Dolf that explains his famous saying, "The Deal of the Decade comes along about once a week."

Dolf's Deal of the Decade

When Dolf was at university, the garage for his house was at the end of a long drive. Every time he drove to class, and every time he came home, he looked at the overgrown weeds and the poor condition of the paint of the house next door. He was annoyed that it looked so horrible. Twice a day for more than a year, he mentally cursed the neighbors for pulling down the value of his property. The neighbor's house had been for sale at $26,000 for that entire time. One day he noticed someone mowing the weeds and painting the house. He was thrilled that someone had bought it and was making the place look better. Three weeks later it sold for $86,000.

At the time, Dolf was on annual student grant of $3,000. Sixty thousand dollars profit, minus the cost of some paint and petrol for the mower, was a fortune. And yet, instead of seeing the potential profit, he had cursed the ugly state of the house next door twice a day for more than a year. If your theory is that people should keep their properties looking good, you'll have lots of reason to complain. But if you see these ugly houses as opportunities, then you'll see good deals all around.

This was a great lesson for Dolf. Since then he's developed the theory that the Deal of the Decade comes along about once a week. And guess what—he's always finding evidence to support his theory.

The deals are still out there. Somewhere, someone is taking advantage of the Deal of the Decade. When is it your turn? When would *now* be a good time?

The Insider's Guide to Making Money in Real Estate

Three ways to read this book:

- Go to Appendix B, and read the Short Version of This Book. Perfect if you want to impress your friends with how fast you can read a book.
- Read the book the old-fashioned way. Perfect if you want to increase your knowledge about real estate investing.
- Read the Short Version first, read the book the old-fashioned way, and do each of the Action Steps along the way. Perfect if you are really serious about real estate investing and are ready to take action to change your financial life.

Whatever path you choose, enjoy your journey!

PART ONE

Fundamentals of Real Estate

Chapter 1

REAL VALID REASONS WHY YOU CAN'T MAKE MONEY IN REAL ESTATE

REASONS WHY YOU CAN'T INVEST
IN REAL ESTATE

I don't have time for real estate.

There are no good deals left.

I don't know if a property is a good deal.

I don't know how to get started.

I live in an area where the mortgage payment is greater than the rental income.

The prices are too high where I live.

I can't sleep at night if I have too much debt.

I need to have a job in order to get a loan.

I must have 20 percent or more down to buy property.

I have bad credit. I could never get a loan.

There is a real estate bubble. The values are going to go down.

I know someone who really got burned in real estate.

I don't want to deal with tenants.

Real estate is slow.

I don't have any money to get started.

I have credit card debt.

I'm too young.

I'm too old.

CAN YOU RELATE?

People all over the world give us the same excuses for not having invested in real estate. However, these aren't real reasons at all. They are, in fact, myths—*wealth myths*.

The beliefs feel so real because they have an element of truth. But, for a moment, consider an alternative way of looking at these negative beliefs. If we take the nugget of truth and strip it of the false assumptions surrounding it, then there will be no limit to what you can achieve. Nothing great has ever been achieved without overcoming something. Or, to paraphrase a favorite saying—if it were easy, everybody would be doing it.

Let's examine some of these common excuses and strip them of their myths.

I don't have time for real estate.

Time is the only thing that we are all given in equal quantity and proportion. We may be blessed with varying levels of talent, intellect, drive, and physical prowess. But, all of us are given exactly 24 hours a day. The fundamental thing that sets successful people apart is how they use their 24 hours.

Seen in this light, the common lament "I wish I had more time" (as opposed to "I wish I had more intelligence and drive") seems all the more pathetic. You can wish, but you're not going to get it! It's what you do with your time that matters.

If you knew, beyond doubt, that you could make $20 million over the next 10 years putting in just three hours per week, would you find the time? Life is all about priorities. We know that even modest amounts of time can lead to significant wealth creation. The three hours you spend watching television this week may be costing you millions!

There are no good deals left.

Have you ever noticed that when you have a theory, you will always find evidence to support it? People who truly believe that there are no good deals left will always find evidence to support that theory. If you believe strongly enough that there are no good deals, you will have to settle for lousy deals.

These days, more than ever before, people are mobile. We move because of new jobs, new families, divorce, marriage, death, and just general changes in our life. In fact, the average American moves every five to six years. This means that more than 8 million homes are bought and sold every year. Many of these will be great deals.

Now, here is the best news of all: You don't need to find the good deals yourself. Who will do so for you? We call them real estate agents.

I don't know if a property is a good deal.

If you look at one deal all by itself, it will be hard to know if it's a good deal. In fact, if you look at only one deal, you could easily make a bad decision. Look at many properties. Read the classified ads. Search for properties on the Internet. Talk with other investors. And, of course, consult with real estate agents—they are looking at deals all day long. That's how you learn to smell a good deal before even seeing the property.

A good deal may have a large positive cash flow, high potential for appreciation, unique tax benefits, large amount of land, possibility for use change, or any combination of these and countless other factors that can make an otherwise mediocre deal extraordinary. Part of the trick is to leave emotions out of the decision-making process. Don't buy a house just because it's cute, or the neighbor's dog is cute or, for that matter, the neighbor is cute.

The more you know about the area trends and demographics, the easier it will be to spot a great deal. When you've spotted a deal that seems great, it's time to do some analysis. Analysis is something that is best done in the cold light of day. And at this point, you still don't need to have seen the property! In fact, we have both bought properties without ever viewing them. Investing in real estate is all about the numbers.

I don't know how to get started.

To borrow a phrase, "Just do it!" Put this book down right now! Pick up a newspaper or go to the Internet and look for a good deal. What comes up for you? Do you not know if it's a good location? Or do you not know what the cash flow returns are? Or do you not know how to calculate before- and after-tax returns? Whatever comes up for you is what you need to learn next.

We don't want this book to be a theoretical guide about what you might do *if* you ever decided to be a real estate investor. Instead we want this to be a practical handbook to guide you through the selection, acquisition, financing, and management stages of owning real estate.

I live in an area where the mortgage payment is greater than the rental income.

We love this myth because we have not just one, but three solutions.

First, if it's true that the average house in an area won't cash flow (appreciation has outpaced rental increases), remember that it is an average. This book is not about being average—it's about how to find the extraordinary among the ordinary. If you look long and hard enough you will find a property where the sales price is low in relation to the rent or where the rent is currently below market. In other words, the mere act of bringing rents up to market levels may allow the property to cash flow.

Second, even if it does not cash flow as is, what can be done to the property to increase rents? For example, if you have a two-bedroom, one-bathroom home in an area of three-bedroom, two-bathroom homes, does it make sense to upgrade the property? The increased rents may well more than cover the increased mortgage payments.

Similarly, you might be able to turn a property with negative cash flow into one with positive cash flow by:

Adding a swimming pool.

Adding a garage or carport.

Changing the zoning.

Adding high-speed Internet.

Putting in an alarm.

Painting.

Or . . . any of countless other things that can be done that have high perceived value in relation to actual cost.

Third, look somewhere else. If you are buying your first investment property, we strongly recommend that you buy it near where you live. That's because you will be familiar with the area, you might already know some real estate agents, and it will be easy to look at the property. In fact, you might want to buy the first several properties near where you live. But at some point, especially if you live where it's hard to find positive cash flow properties, you might want to diversify into other areas.

The prices are too high where I live.

What a great problem to have! High prices indicate high appreciation in the past. And that's one of the indicators for what might happen in the future.

Furthermore, everything is likely to be in proportion. Banks will lend more, seller carrybacks will be higher, and the rents you collect will also be more. The value of improvements will be higher as well. For example, building a $30,000 pool on a $100,000 home might increase the value by only $15,000. But, building that $30,000 pool on a million-dollar property might increase the value by $50,000.

Get used to big numbers. Remember, $25,000 sounded like a lot in 1968, but back then that was just the average home price.

I can't sleep at night if I have too much debt.

Debt can be your friend, or your enemy. Debt secured against assets that decline in value such as stereo equipment, shoes, and cars is risky. But, debt secured against assets that go up in value (and where the asset generates income that more than covers the payment) can build wealth. In both cases, debt means leverage. If the underlying asset goes down in value, you get poor faster. If the underlying asset goes up in value, you get rich faster.

Apart from the extra leverage and financial gain advantages, debt protects the owner while equity protects the lender. For example, if you have a property worth $400,000 and you owe $300,000, you have only $100,000 in equity at risk from frivolous lawsuits, bad tenants, and even foreclosure. However, if you have that same property worth $400,000 and you owe $100,000, you now have $300,000 at risk. High levels of debt give you more leverage and asset protection.

In fact, perhaps the worst thing you can do is to make extra principal payments on your loan. The extra payments don't help you if you miss a payment—the bank just gets more equity if they foreclose. Additionally, you've relinquished the financial boon of leverage.

I need to have a job in order to get a loan.

If you are told (and you will be) that you must have a job in order to get a loan, then you need to ask someone else. For example, there are three different types of conventional lenders: (1) banks and other lending institutions, (2) mortgage brokers, and (3) mortgage bankers. A loan processor is someone who works for one particular lending institution (often a bank) and understands one or two different types of loan programs. Loan processors work primarily with employees. Mortgage brokers, however, work with different lenders and so can offer numerous choices. Mortgage bankers put their own lending programs together by providing private investors. They have the most flexibility of all.

I must have 20 percent or more down to buy property.

There are many people who think that in order to do a 100 percent financed deal you must get a single loan for 100 percent of the purchase price. If that's your belief, and you can't get such a mortgage, then you will indeed feel stuck. However, 100 percent financing does not have to be a single mortgage. For example, you could get a first mortgage of 70 percent and a second mortgage of 30 percent. Or you could be bold and ask the seller to leave some money in. If you get an 80 percent mortgage and the seller agrees to lend you 20 percent (sometimes called seller carryback), then that property is still 100 percent financed.

Furthermore, 100 percent financing does not mean that you must offer the property being bought for 100 percent of the collateral. There is nothing to stop you from borrowing 80 percent against the property you're buying and borrowing the remaining 20 percent against another property—maybe even your existing home. Even though you are using your home for part of the funding, the property you are buying is still 100 percent financed. You could also use a loan from Aunt Murgatroid, a credit card, an outside investor, or a combination of any of the above to enable you to buy a property without having to contribute even $1 of cash.

I have bad credit. I could never get a loan.

The better your credit rating, the easier it will be to get a loan. Having said that, very few people have perfect credit. If you have less than perfect credit, you will have to work a little bit harder to get the loan. And any steps taken to improve your credit will make it easier next time.

If you have bad credit now and it is absolutely impossible for you to get a loan in your own name, use the credit of someone else! Perhaps the easiest way to do that is to use the seller's credit by getting them to stay on the mortgage.

If you have bad credit now, do you want to retire with bad credit? You can get a copy of your credit report and check what is causing your credit score to be bad. If you have too much *bad debt* such as revolving credit cards, what can you do to fix that? If you have too much *open credit* (revolving credit cards with zero balances), contact the issuing company to cancel some. That action alone can dramatically improve your credit rating. If you have past-due bills, work out a payment plan that includes removing the bad score from your credit report.

The outcome is to make you fabulously rich through real estate. If you are struggling with $5,000, $10,000 or $15,000 in credit card debt, you'll never get there. You need to learn to be in control of your finances, and that often starts with your credit cards.

What if there is a real estate bubble? Will values go down?

Chances are values will go down at some stage, but when might that happen? Do you want to forgo catching an 80 percent increase in value to avoid a potential 10 percent downturn? Values do not go up in a straight line. Rather, they go up in fits and starts. Sometimes they even go down. In general, though, at the end of each cycle, each peak is higher than the previous peak and each trough is higher than the previous trough.

I know someone who really got burned in real estate.

We all know someone who bought a car that turned out to be a lemon. Many of us have bought tickets to a movie that we walked out of. And chances are most of us have eaten at a restaurant and regretted it a few hours later. But that doesn't stop us from buying cars, going to the movies, or eating out. If you take a thousand people at random who buy cars, go to movies, or eat at restaurants, you will find a lot of dissatisfaction. But if you survey a thousand people at random who have bought real estate, most will be heard to bemoan, "If only I'd bought more."

Real estate is very forgiving of mistakes. What's more, you can improve your odds for success by buying smart, financing well, and managing with integrity.

I don't want to deal with tenants.

Real estate works because you have tenants who make the payments for you. In the long run, it is the capital appreciation that will generate the big dollars. But, in the mean time, it's because you have tenants who pay rent that you can even play the game. Seen in this light, tenants are your clients. Be grateful for them.

If you still don't want to deal with tenants, we recommend that you engage a property manager. Hiring a good property manager will enable you to concentrate on building your real estate portfolio.

Real estate is slow.

Isn't it wonderful that you don't need to watch your portfolio day by day like you do with stocks, hour by hour like you do with futures contracts, or minute by minute like you do with currency markets? Real estate keeps chugging along, making you richer each year. If you have four people on a cruise boat—a real estate investor, a stock broker, a futures trader, and a currency trader, how often do they have to check in and how frustrated are they when they lose communication with shore? As the cruise goes on, the real estate investor gets more and more relaxed while the other three get more and more frustrated. We once heard of a stock trader who went on a cruise and at the end, found out that his satellite phone bill was larger than the cost of the cruise! Real estate is slow—delightfully slow. It is the slow-but-sure way to wealth.

I don't have any money to get started.

If you don't have money to get started, then you'll have to start without money. Any fool with a million dollars in the bank can buy a property worth a half million. Someone who has no money is going to have to work a little harder and a little smarter to buy that same property. But, it is possible. That's one of the reasons that we like real estate so much.

Try getting started in stocks, bonds, mutual funds, or 401(k) plans without any money. Your sanity will be questioned.

I have credit card debt.

There are three ways you can deal with credit card debt: (1) Let it continue to build and do nothing, (2) put your life on hold until it's paid off, or (3) learn the lessons from the debt you've accumulated and make changes today.

If your solution is to deal with the credit card debt, then read on. Some people advocate cutting up your credit cards. We strongly disagree! Debt is your friend; the key is to learn how to manage it. In fact, credit cards can actually give you benefits in the form of airline mileage awards. Diane and her husband Richard personally charge everything to their credit cards and then pay them off each month. The average return, based on the value of airline tickets, is 4.9 percent. So, the problem isn't the credit cards, it's what you do with them.

First, make the promise to yourself to continue to carry the credit cards and to not use them. Appreciate the fact that this requires self-discipline about money, a critical element of being a successful real estate investor.

Now, go back and investigate why you have the debt in the first place. Is it due to nonessential purchases? Learning to delay gratification is one of the most significant steps to being a long-term investor. Or, learn to reward yourself with a piece of property instead of a new car. The car will depreciate and won't pay you back. The property can create a cash flow that can buy the car.

Or, perhaps, the debt came about because of real emergencies. If that's the case, then you desperately need to have a liquid emergency account. Establish that immediately so that you never have to go to credit cards again when life's emergencies occur.

After you are certain that you control the credit cards, and not the other way around, you might consider investing. It isn't always necessary to first pay the credit card debt off—in fact the income from the real estate can help you do that!

The secret, though, is to first discover why you have the credit card debt. Until you have real solutions to the real problem, stay out of real estate. Credit card debt isn't stopping you. Not understanding how and when to use debt is stopping you.

I'm too young.

We've heard "I'm too young" from people approaching 30. Yet, we've also talked to investors who had been investing for years before they hit their thirtieth birthday. In fact, we both had been investing for years before we were 30. So, if 30 is not too young, then what about 25? What about 22? Maybe there is no point at which you are actually too young to begin investing in real estate, provided you are capable of rational thought. It really is just a mindset.

Of all the objections in this chapter, this is the one that is the most subjective. It comes from within, rather than from without. We'll boldly say that you're never too young.

I'm too old.

We were at a closing once where our client had to excuse himself to find a battery for his hearing aid. Then, he left his reading glasses where he had found his battery and couldn't read the closing documents. (Of course, the battery had been replaced in his hearing aid, so he could hear us read it to him.) And, what's more, he had just gotten new dentures and his teeth didn't fit very well. It was hard for us to understand what he might have been objecting to. But, in the end, he bought the property.

We'll boldly say that you're never too old.

WHAT'S STOPPING YOU?

Real estate seems so intimidating that most people are afraid to get started. Yet these same people know they can buy a stereo or a car on credit and do so without even thinking twice. Banks want to lend you money. Think about it—that's their business. In fact, looking at it from an accountant's perspective, a bank deposit is a liability and a loan is an asset. If a bank is sitting on money and not lending it out, it is doing its shareholders a disservice. If you don't have great credit, you might have to shop around a little bit or go to "hard money" sources, but you can still find money.

Perhaps the biggest reason people don't get into real estate is because they don't know how to spot a deal. The sensational deals come into play when you can identify problems and know how to turn them into opportunities.

If you are still convinced that you can't buy real estate, then you can't. Equally, if you believe that you can find great real estate deals, you will, through the sheer force of knowledge and determination, create an empire that will fulfill your wildest dreams. The choice is up to you.

FINAL WORD

You don't need to invest in real estate to be wealthy. But, by and large, it's the easiest, most leveraged method to build real, sustainable wealth. And, the field is open to everyone. You don't need any more education. You don't need any more money. You don't need any more credit. It's all waiting for you. The choice is yours. What will you do with the opportunity before you? We wish you the best of luck.

Chapter 2

WHY REAL ESTATE?

WHY REAL ESTATE?

If you've bought this book, chances are you're looking for ways to make money. You might be intrigued with the idea of a passive income stream, or income that works when you don't want to, or perhaps you just relish the idea of telling your boss "I quit!" some day soon. Maybe you're experiencing the feeling of "I don't want to miss out" as you hear about the success stories of other real estate investors, or it could be that you're already a successful real estate investor and are looking for the "insider's tips" to take your current investing to another level. No matter what level you are currently at, or what outcome you want from your real estate investing, the benefits you get will be directly related

32

to how much you utilize all the wealth-building attributes of real estate.

Owning real estate is not the only way to get rich. However, it is an easy way to begin building wealth. And real estate investing is the easiest way we know to build wealth using the principles of leverage and taking full advantage of legal tax loopholes.

WHY REAL ESTATE IS BETTER THAN STOCKS

The beauty of real estate is that it offers several opportunities for leverage, something that the stock market does not. For example, say you have $20,000 to invest, and you are trying to determine which would be a better investment. Let's take a look at your options.

Option 1: You find a property in a borderline neighborhood that is close enough to town that it could become gentrified. The property is run down and costs only $150,000. You put down a 10 percent deposit of $15,000, and plan to spend the other $5,000 on upgrades.

Option 2: You invest $20,000 in the stock market, $10,000 in blue-chip stocks and the other $10,000 in an aggressive mutual fund that is targeting biochemical ventures.

Now let's go forward in time—not far, just a month. Let's see where our two investments stand:

Option 1: The upgrades have been done and the house has been rented for enough money to pay your mortgage, insurance, and all other monthly expenses associated with the property. You now have a financially independent asset that cost $155,000, but is really worth much more! Based on your smart assessment of other values in the area, you knew that the $5,000 you put into upgrades would give you a property worth $175,000 when you were done. You now have total equity of $40,000 from your initial $20,000 investment. We call that "active appreciation."

Option 2: The blue-chip stocks haven't really moved. The biochemical ventures fund has risen by 10 percent. You now have stocks worth $22,000.

Do you see what happened here? By leveraging your money into a down payment you have secured an asset that is self-sufficient—it's paying for itself without any more immediate input from you—and your $20,000 is now worth $40,000. The stock market, on the other hand, doesn't have those same opportunities to leverage. If you want to buy $20,000 worth of stock, you need to have $20,000 to start with. Hopefully your investment will increase along with the stock value. But even if it does, you'll be waiting a long time to see the same level of profit you got from your property after only one month. That's the beauty of leverage. Yes, you used $15,000 of your own money to purchase the property. But you used $135,000 of someone else's money. And what's more, because the property is renting out for slightly more than it's costing you to cover the mortgage, insurance, and so forth, you're making a profit on someone else's money.

Here's an idea to think about. What do you think would be more likely—getting a mortgage loan from your bank manager or getting a personal loan from your bank manager so that you can go and play the stock market? Even if you are buying blue-chip stocks with the loan, there is still no guarantee that those stocks won't crash at some point and be worthless. The property that you purchase, however, will still be there and is far less likely to lose money that the stocks. There is nothing intangible about real property. It's right there, on the street, pink, purple, blue, green trim, white trim, French windows, Cape Cod shutters, and so on. Your bank manager can drive by and see it for himself or herself every day after work. You can use the property as collateral for the loan money. You can't necessarily do that with the stock market. Have you ever noticed that there are considerably more advertisements in the newspaper, on television, or in your e-mail in-box offering mortgage finance than there are advertisements offering you money to invest in the stock market? Why do you think that is? And, why do you think the rates are so much lower for mortgages than they are for personal loans? Property is a safe investment from a bank's perspective. And the safer the investment, the more likely your bank manager is to look at you, smile, and write a check.

Here's another idea. What do you think is more likely—that you locate an undervalued property, or that you locate an undervalued biochemical stock? There are many reasons why a property may be undervalued. We live in a society that loves instant gratification. For some people, selling the house and moving on is just another item on a long list that is waiting to be crossed off. As long as the offer is reasonable, and you can close quickly, they'll take it, in the interest of moving along. Estate sales and divorce sales are two other areas where you can often find a bargain. A family member, who has little or no property background, charged with disposing of Grandmother's estate, may be more inclined to take a lower offer to get the place sold than a savvy real estate agent would. And for a couple divorcing, the end cannot possibly come soon enough.

Now, what about stock? Sure, there can be great reasons for it to be undervalued. There might be research in the works that will pay off in the end. There might be a company lurking out there that wants to take over the undervalued company. However, in many cases it's going to be much harder to figure out which stock is undervalued and which isn't. If the company has released information about its research, you need to be able to understand what it is doing, and why it will be successful. That's assuming that you can get hold of all of the information, which isn't always the case. With real estate, on the other hand, it's much easier for you to find a bargain.

And for yet another angle, let's go the opposite way. Which do you think you are more likely to come across—an overvalued property or an overvalued stock? Of course there are overvalued properties, especially in very hot real estate markets. A buying frenzy in one particular geographical area can push property prices out of reason very quickly. As an inexperienced real estate investor, you may be afraid that you will be the one to buy the bad deal and have everything go wrong, especially right now, with the intense popularity of real estate investing in the United States. However, this is also an area where you might find yourself getting help in sorting deal from disaster from an unlikely source—your bank manager. Remember, your banker has a vested interest in your success, and probably has a lot more experience than you, especially in your early days. Your banker is likely to put the brakes on a lemon. Of course, appraisers, real estate agents and property managers can also help you make a lucid decision.

As for overvalued stocks, well, that story speaks for itself. Between March 2000 and October 2002, during the dot-com crash, the Nasdaq composite fell by 78 percent from 5046.86 to 1114.11. Since that time the American public has had to deal with multiple instances of stock manipulation and outright fraud, both on the part of major public companies and by stockbrokers and stock promoters.

When was the last time you saw a piece of real estate lose 78 percent of its value? And when was the last time one of your advisors hyped an overpriced piece of real estate because he or she stood to gain personally?

Okay, let's go back to the beginning of this discussion, back to you and your $20,000 initial investment. One of the things that you did with your property was to spend $5,000 on renovations, which enabled you to get a tenant paying enough in rent to cover your mortgage and all of your other property-related expenses. Now, could you do the same thing with your $20,000 stock market investment? Spend a bit more money and enhance the value of your stock market investment?

The answer is no. As a stockholder of a public company, you have very little control over the business of that company. The key business decisions are all going to be made by the officers and directors of that corporation. You, as an investor, are left with two options—sell your stock, or have faith in the company. You could spend another $5,000, but all you would get for your money was another $5,000 in stock.

Here's one final thought on why real estate is better than stock. Let's say that the neighborhood saw a general increase in values, and your $150,000 house (which you turned into a $175,000 house) has appreciated to a $250,000 home. And, let's also say that your $20,000 stock investment has also appreciated, and is now worth $28,000. How can you access some of the profits without disturbing anything?

With your real estate, the answer is pretty simple. By refinancing your mortgage loan, you can withdraw plenty of equity—after all, you've seen great appreciation—and use that money for all sorts of things, from a trip to Mauritius to a co-op in Manhattan. And, because you have so much equity in your property, you will very likely be able to finance on better terms than you originally received. Plus, your tenant is still there, the property is still turning a profit, and you are still leveraging someone else's money. In fact, once you refinance you'll likely be turning an even greater profit, especially if your loan costs are reduced with the new financing!

With your stock investment, the answer is not quite as satisfying. To get money out of your investment, you're going to have to sell some of it. You'll have to pay taxes on what you sell, of course. And, you'll wind up with a smaller investment and that means less future profit.

Can you make money with stocks? Of course you can. But, we maintain that it will take more diligent study and harder work to find the best niches in the highly competitive stock market. Real estate is slow but steady. To be honest, it's even a little boring at times. But, it's how both of the authors have made and kept their wealth.

BENEFITS FROM REAL ESTATE

There are actually four benefits you can receive from real estate:

1. Passive appreciation.
2. Active appreciation.
3. Cash flow.
4. Tax benefits.

PASSIVE APPRECIATION

Passive appreciation means the property goes up in value without your help. Dolf frequently tells his sellout seminar attendees his personal insider's secret to maximizing passive appreciation. In the United States, property, on average, appreciated by approximately 9 percent last year. If you want better-than-average results, look for areas that historically have had better-than-average growth. For example, here is a sampling of appreciation rates per state from the Office of Federal Housing Oversight:

House Price Appreciation by State
Percentage Change in House Prices for the
Period Ended June 30, 2004

State	1-Year % Change	5-Year % Change	% Change Since 1980
Nevada	22.92	53.06	183.37
Hawaii	18.90	53.79	255.49
California	18.39	84.10	338.72
Rhode Island	17.86	87.78	383.92
District of Columbia	16.07	95.10	316.06
Florida	14.23	61.28	208.96
New Jersey	12.75	64.97	329.40
New Hampshire	10.39	71.13	318.61
Massachusetts	9.79	73.38	528.62
United States	**9.36**	**43.59**	**218.03**
Michigan	3.99	27.86	205.42
Indiana	3.05	18.20	138.67

To be updated on the latest trends in appreciation, for free, please register at our web site, www.DolfAndDiane.com.

Neighborhood Appreciation

Not only do some states have higher appreciation rates than others, but within states, some cities have higher appreciation rates than others. For instance, in California (a highly appreciating state in its own right), San Francisco, Los Angeles, and San Diego typically appreciate at a much higher rate than Eureka, Lodi, or Thermal Grasshopper.

Similarly, property often appreciates at different rates within different neighborhoods in a city. To find an area on the upswing, drive around and look for signs of rehabilitation.

Signs That a Neighborhood Is Improving

- More than 10 percent of homes in the neighborhood are getting new roofs.
- Large industrial dumpsters in front of buildings.
- Freshly painted buildings.
- New evidence of landscaping.

You might also see a number of "For Sale" signs as you drive around a neighborhood. This isn't necessarily a bad thing. If values have gone up significantly, the For Sale signs might be evidence of some profit-takers selling to take advantage of the increase. It could also mean that there is something bad happening, or about to happen, in the neighborhood. A large number of For Sale signs means something is going on, but don't jump to conclusions on what that might mean. The one thing you can be certain of is that it might mean you will have a lot of competition if you buy a property for a quick sale.

If you are buying a property to generate a quick sale, though, be aware of new house construction in the area. It is often hard to sell an older house in a market where there are new houses with new warranties available for potential purchases. Generally, the only benefit that an older house can offer would be charm (and it would have to be a substantially older house to have that) or good landscaping.

ACTIVE APPRECIATION

You're already familiar with active appreciation, and might not even know it. Active appreciation comes about when a property goes up in value with some outside help by way of fixing it up. Some examples of active appreciation are:

- Updating a house.
- Constructing a garage.
- Putting in landscaping.
- Cleaning the property.
- Painting the property.
- Changing zoning for better use.

One of Diane's favorite examples of active appreciation concerns one of her office buildings in Phoenix. Diane and her husband bought the house when it was a single-family residence in historic Phoenix for $239,000. In fact, they paid full price for the property. That's because the property had zoning on it that would allow conversion to professional offices, which is exactly what they did. With the change in use, the property was suddenly worth $329,000! An appraisal provided the value. They immediately refinanced the property and took out money, tax free, to use for other investments. And, Diane's offices are still partially housed in this great little historic Craftsman bungalow in downtown Phoenix.

Tips for Improving Your Residential Properties

- Dress up the front of the property (flowers, paint, a brightly painted door).
- Clean up both the inside and the outside of the property.
- Update the house with new carpet, floor coverings, and paint.
- Change the sensory perceptions (for example, make it smell good).
- Add a garage or carport, if appropriate for your area.
- Change knobs on the kitchen cabinets to modernize.
- Install an alarm.
- Tear down a rusty shed.

In fact, Dolf is so excited about how easy it is to create value that he's written a book full of ideas on how to make changes entitled *101 Ways to Massively Increase the Value of Your Real Estate Without Spending Much Money*.

Multifamily and commercial properties generally see increased value due to increased cash flow and profitability. Increased cash flow usually means increased rents and other sources of income. While it is possible to stop fixing things as a way to increase the bottom line, we do not recommend deferring maintenance as a way to raise the cash flow on a property.

> ### Tips for Quickly Improving the Value of Your Multifamily and Commercial Properties
>
> - Add storage units.
> - Add coin-operated laundry.
> - Increase rents (if they are currently under market value).
> - Fill vacancies by first determining *why* the vacancies exist.
> - Change primary tenant focus to create more value.
> - Split a large vacant space into smaller rentable areas.

Target Tenant Needs

In today's highly appreciating markets, it's become harder to find properties that create positive cash flow. One strategy is to look for ways that you can change the use to generate higher rental income. At the same time, you'll often create active appreciation as well.

In college towns, student housing is often in high demand. The Arizona State University (ASU) campus in Tempe, Arizona, is no exception. Recently, a resourceful contractor purchased a multifamily unit consisting solely of tiny one-bedroom apartments near the campus. The units were dark and outdated, so the property didn't sell at a high price. Other investors had looked at the property and by the time they factored in the high cost of renovating all of the kitchens (as well as new floor coverings, paint, and the bathroom renovations) it just didn't make sense. The resourceful contractor had another idea, though. He bought the building and then combined the apartments into larger units. Three former one-bedroom apartments were combined to make three suites with a large common area with one kitchen, one living room, and one family room. Instead of renting the one-bed-room units for $450 per month, he now gets $1,100 per month for each suite because he had done such a great job with the renovation. Yet, the renovation was significantly cheaper because he had only redone one-third of the kitchens (often the most expensive part of a remodel). He ended up refinancing to take all of his invested cash out and now has passive cash flow of over $5,000 per month. And, the property is worth a lot more too!

PROPERTY VALUE IS UP, NOW WHAT?

With both active and passive appreciation, you are left with the question of what to do now that the property has gone up in value. It's really tempting to sell and take the cash. If you believe that the property might decline in value, it might make sense to sell. You can sell the property either outright or by carrying the note. If you have held the property for less than a year, you will pay tax on any capital gain at your marginal income tax rate. If you have held the property for over one year, you will pay tax on any gain at the current capital gains tax rate. You will also have to recapture previously taken depreciation and pay tax at a higher tax rate for that portion.

Alternatively, you could also sell the property through a Section 1031 exchange. This is also known as a Starker exchange or like-kind exchange. You will be able to roll over your basis in the property into another property, thus deferring the tax on the gain. You must identify another property within 45 days from the date of sale and close on a property within 180 days. You cannot take any cash from the initial sale and you must purchase a property worth at least as much as the property you sold to fully qualify for the tax deferral.

Even better, if the property still produces cash flow or is in an area that is appreciating (or is likely to begin appreciating again), don't sell! Instead, refinance the property to take out the equity. The interest on the additional funds will still be tax-deductible as long as you've reinvested the money. If you take the extra money for personal use, the interest won't be tax-deductible. But, regardless of the deductibility of the interest, you will still have the property plus you've freed up the cash that was "trapped" within the equity.

CASH FLOW

Cash flow from the property is crucial for you to pay property tax, interest, maintenance, and other expenses. In the case of real estate, cash flow is generated by rent. Cash flow is not the only sign of a good property investment. Since vacant land generally doesn't have rental income, it is not even an investment under this definition. For the same reason, banks are reluctant to lend money secured against vacant land. And even if they did, then the mortgage interest as well as other costs of the property (property tax, weed control, insurance, improvements) are not currently tax deductible. This is because the property must be generating taxable income before expenses can be claimed as a tax deduction.

Every property has cash flow. The question really is, "Which way is the cash flowing?" Is it flowing to you, or to the bank? If the cash comes to you each and every month, you have a positive cash flow. The other direction is called negative cash flow.

It is good practice to estimate the cash flow from a prospective property before you buy. We recommend that you estimate the cash flow with the following formula:

Rent (based on numbers you have verified yourself).
Less: Vacancy (use vacancy rates that are common for
             your area).
        Insurance.
        Property management fees.
        Property tax.
        Repairs.
        Utilities.

Conduct a Rent Survey

- *When?* Conduct a rent survey before you make an offer on a property and periodically after you have bought a property.
- *Why?* To ensure that you are charging market rents for your property or that you have used market rents in your projections.
- *Who?* The best person to conduct a rent survey is you (or someone you really trust).
- *How?* Knock on a few doors in the neighborhood and ask, "What do you think I would pay in rent for an apartment (or house) like this in this neighborhood?"
- Some reputable property managers may also give fair market rent advice.

Rent

Unfortunately, this is one of the areas that might get a little puffed up in the sales process. You'll find some pro-formas (estimated profit and loss statements) that are given by anxious sellers showing what rents *should be*, instead of what they actually are. Of course, the real question is, "Why are the rents not at these optimistic levels as quoted in the pro-forma?"

Do yourself a favor and check out the rents by doing a rent survey. The best way to do a rent survey is to go knock on a few doors.

Vacancy

The vacancy factor is the best guess of how often the property would be vacant. Vacancy often has a bigger cost than just the loss of rent, though. If you have a lot of turnover in a property, you will spend more money on maintenance items. Often a unit will need to be painted after every tenant moves out, for example.

Insurance

Insurance costs are on the rise. Make sure the pro-forma you see for the property shows an increase in this cost from the previous year. It's also a good idea to see the past insurance history for the property. Unfortunately, prior claims can affect the insurability of the property when you purchase. Check this out before you buy. You can order a report of past claims, called a C.L.U.E. report, from www.choicetrust.com.

Property Management Fees

Unless you are planning to work for free, there will be a cost associated with managing the property. Some people try to "trick" the numbers by volunteering their time to manage and maintain the property. That's not a bad idea, but there is a cost to doing that. One of the costs will be that you are limiting how much other work you can do (such as looking for your next deal). You might soon discover that the three most expensive words in the English language are "Do it yourself."

Property Tax

The property tax cost is an easy one to check out. Verify the estimated property tax amount is correct by checking with the Assessor's Office.

Repairs

If there's a problem with the pro-forma, it will be in one of two areas: rentals or repairs. Have a property inspector check the property prior to purchase as part of your due diligence. The few hundreds of dollars that the inspector will cost (up to $1,000 or more if it is a large multiunit project) could very well save you many times that amount. There are generally two parts to the repair cost: (1) deferred maintenance that previous owners didn't handle and (2) ongoing maintenance costs. Your inspector can likely help you estimate the cost of the deferred maintenance. The repair costs on an annual basis will vary based on the part of the country in which the property is located and the age of the building. For example, air conditioners need to be replaced after just five years of use in Phoenix, whereas weather damage due to snow will cause excess expenses in the northeast. Talk to other real estate investors to get a handle on maintenance costs or talk to an advisor who has other real estate investor clients.

The point of all of these calculations is to estimate the cash flow from a prospective property before you buy. Use it as the beginning estimated budget to refine your calculations if you buy. Compare the estimates to the real numbers to get better numbers for the future estimates. Go to Figure 9.1 for an easy-to-use form that summarizes all of the above information on just one page. You can also check out software to analyze real estate at www.DolfAndDiane.com.

TAX BENEFITS

The government *wants* you to be a real estate investor! That's why there are so many tax advantages (called *loopholes*) available to the investor. There are three main areas of tax benefits available to the serious real estate investor:

1. Tax deductions.
2. Depreciation.
3. Tax credits.

Note that we said "serious" investors. The U.S. tax law limits the amount of tax deductions that you can take from your real estate to just $25,000 of loss if your income is under $100,000. Above $100,000 the loss amount phases out until your income exceeds $150,000, at which point no loss is allowed at all. The loophole is the real estate professional status. If you're a real estate professional, then 100 percent of your real estate loss, no matter how much, is allowed against your other income, no matter how much it is.

You might be wondering why we're talking about real estate losses. After all, you're investing in real estate to create income, not loss. That's one of the wonderful things about real estate. You can actually have cash every month that you put in your pocket and still, legally, show a tax loss, that gets claimed (deducted!) against other income.

TAX DEDUCTIONS

There are two things that the government wants you to do: (1) Start businesses and (2) Invest in real estate. If you do one or both of those things, you will be rewarded with government-sanctioned loopholes. Can you imagine what it would be like to know that you're making more money than ever before and paying less tax and doing it all with the government's blessing?

Many people find it hard to start a business, but investing in real estate is more passive. It still requires some work, especially in the beginning, but it is more achievable for most people than most other wealth-building techniques. Now, here's the good news. Real estate investing is also a business. You can now take advantage of all of the tax benefits that are available to the business owner.

That can be a big change for someone who has always been an employee, used to following the "Earn-Tax-Spend" syndrome of the employee, where you earn money, pay tax on it, and then spend what's left. As a business owner, you can take advantage of legal tax loopholes to use the "Earn-Spend-Tax" solution of the business owner, where you earn money, then spend on legitimate deductions, and pay tax on what's left. In other words, there are some items that you can pay for with before-tax money. Here are the five most common business deductions for real estate investors.

Kids

If you've got kids, we're sure you'll agree that they do cost money. You can pay some of those expenses with before-tax money by employing them to perform tasks for your business. These need to be legitimate tasks that are age-appropriate. For example, you can hire your 12-year-old son to file paperwork for your business, but it isn't reasonable to hire your 6-month-old daughter to put up a web site.

Legally Employ Your Child in Your Business

Follow these three rules for proper record-keeping when you employ your child in your business.

1. Have a written job description for your child.
2. Your child should keep a time slip or worksheet showing hours worked.
3. Pay a reasonable wage for work performed.

Real Estate Travel

Real estate is everywhere! That means that there are opportunities everywhere to buy real estate. It also means that there are real, legitimate business deductions for real estate buying trips. You must be serious about being a real estate investor in order to take this deduction. For example, Dolf and Diane both buy real estate around the world. They can both take deductions for the trips to other countries to investigate the real estate market. Even better, they are truly diversifying their real estate investing portfolio by investing outside of the box of traditional home-country investing.

Your travels don't need to be that exotic. It could be simply looking in the state next door to your own home state. Regardless of where the travel is, you must show that you did investigate real estate opportunities while you were there and that you are a serious real estate investor. Keep a journal or make a note in your PDA as to what you saw and the people you met with, and also keep copies of the sales literature and contacts you make when you travel. You can take a deduction only for the business-days portion of the trip, so make every day a business day.

Home Office

The home office is one of those misunderstood and underutilized deductions for businesses. First, let's look at the two requirements for having a legitimate home office deduction. Then, we'll review the little twist to make sure you get this deduction for your real estate investing business.

In order to take the home office deduction, you will need to have a portion of your home used exclusively for business purposes. You can't simply use a corner of the dining room table or the kitchen counter. It needs to be a spot that is used only for business. And, it needs to be a place in which you regularly conduct some kind of business. Those are the two rules: (1) exclusive business use and (2) regularly conducting some kind of business.

Once you have established a legitimate home office expense, you can then take a pro-rata portion of the home-related expenses such as mortgage interest, property tax, insurance, utilities, maintenance, and the like as a deduction. This pro-ration is determined by dividing the square footage of the business use by the total square footage. You can also depreciate a pro-rata portion of the home.

Now, here's the real estate investment twist. If you own property managed by others, then the income would be considered investment income. That means that you would not be able to take advantage of the home office deduction. However, if you actively manage your portfolio by overseeing your property managers and the wealth you are accumulating, that then becomes your business. That means you have the business use requirement covered for your real estate investments.

Auto

Aside from your children and your house, you next biggest expense is likely to be your automobile. Your auto is often a critical part of your real estate investments as well. The business use of the auto is deductible in one of three ways: cents per miles of actual usage, portion of a lease payment, or portion of the actual cost of the vehicle.

Education

A successful real estate investor is always improving her education. Tapes, seminars, magazine subscriptions, real estate

How Do I Deduct My Car?

- Keep a written log for business and personal use for at least three months each year.
- If you lease the car, use the percentage of business use times the payment.
- If you own, is it a current-year purchase that is greater than 6,000 GVW (gross vehicle weight)? If so, you have a special Section 179 deduction that means you can bypass the depreciation requirements.
- If you own it and it doesn't qualify for the special Section 179 deduction, you can take either cents per mile or a percentage of actual use.
- Use the cents per mile method when you put a lot of miles of your vehicle each year and the cost of the auto is relatively small.

investment club dues—they are all deductible. In fact, *the cost of this book* is deductible for a real estate investor. But, did you know that the cost of a public speaking course or motivational seminar is also deductible? If it helps you become more effective in your business of real estate investing, it's going to be deductible. Remember, though, you need to be a serious investor. That means you're really actively involved in real estate. And, you'll need to keep good records of the education that you get and the payments for that education.

DEPRECIATION

We just covered the top deductions for a real estate investor. All of those deductions took after-tax expenses and turned them into before-tax deductions, provided you legitimately have a business and can demonstrate that these expenses were ordinary and necessary for production of income.

Now let's look at a deduction that doesn't cost you any out-of-pocket money. We call it a phantom expense because it's a legitimate tax deduction that doesn't cost you anything! That wonderful phantom expense is *depreciation*. This is the best tax loophole of all for real estate investors. Even though we know that property tends to go up in value (and we call that *appreciation*), the government lets us pretend that it actually

---

Insider Tips for Maximizing Depreciation

- Break out land using the fair market value or assessor's percentage of land versus improvements applied to the basis—whichever is less. The less value in the land, the better for you.
- Break out the value of personal property items in the basis. List these for your accountant.
- When you buy new personal property, clearly separate the value.
- Amortize the cost of tenant improvements in commercial buildings over the life of the tenant's lease.

55

goes down in value over time. In fact, they say, if you have a residential property, it will be worthless in 27.5 years. A commercial property has a little longer life—39 years. By the way, those are the depreciable lives for the building shell. The land is not depreciable. And, the personal property (also called chattels) will be depreciated over shorter lives. Check out www.ChattelAppraisals.com for advice and assistance.

TAX CREDITS

A tax deduction reduces your taxable income. A tax credit is a direct credit of taxes you pay. In other words, a tax credit is the same thing as money in the bank.

There are three major tax credits available to the real estate investor. They are:

1. Americans with Disabilities Act retrofits.
2. Historic building rehabilitation costs.
3. Pre–1936 construction rehabilitation costs.

Retrofitting a property to make it more accessible for handicapped persons under the Americans with Disabilities Act provides a tax credit of up to 50 percent of the costs of the retrofitting. Costs over the yearly limit of $10,500 may be carried forward.

Rehabilitation costs to a historic building may be taken as long as the building retains 75 percent of its exterior walls and looks the same as when it was originally constructed. A tax credit of 10 percent is available for work on buildings constructed prior to 1936, and an additional 10 percent tax credit is available for work on buildings in city, state, or federally designated areas. Combined with ADA retrofitting you could see a 70 percent tax credit on rehabilitation costs.

Now how can you make the real estate benefits even bigger? Chapter 4 will discuss how you can make even more when you take into account the five fundamental wealth-building strategies.

ACTION STEPS

The Insider's Guide to Making Money in Real Estate might look like a book, but we want to let you in on a secret. It's really a guidebook on how you can make money in real estate. Because it's not really a book, we don't want you to just sit back and passively read it. It's not enough to just learn about how real estate and tax laws can immediately put money in your pocket. You need to also be an active participant in creating your own real estate wealth. Now here's the active participation part. Look at the next two categories of action steps. One is for people who already have real estate investment property and the other is for people who do not yet have real estate investment property. Go through the action steps applicable for where you are.

IF YOU OWN PROPERTY:

Complete this for each investment property you own. Do not include your principal residence or any recreational properties. If

(Continued)

(Continued)

you are calling them investments, then they should be included. If they really are luxuries, and not investments, then realize that's part of your lifestyle for which you need to create passive income, or you'll be working for the rest of your life. The choice is yours.

ASSESS WHERE YOU ARE

1. Property name _____

2. Years owned _____

3. Total dollar appreciation since purchase _____

4. Appreciation per year _____

5. Appreciation per year nationally _____

6. How does your property compare? _____

7. Total amount of equity in property _____

8. Check value of comparable properties in the neighborhood. Is there room for active appreciation? How much additional value could you create for the property? What would be the cost to perform the work? Could you raise rents if you performed this work? Can you generate either wealth or cash flow by increasing the value of your property? _____

9. What are three things you could do to improve the cash flow on your property? Remember that improving cash flow means raising rents, finding additional income sources, or reducing expenses.

_____

_____

_____

10. Are you taking advantage of all three tax benefits, where applicable? If not, what can you do right now to begin to put more money in your pocket?

_____

_____

_____

11. Based on the review you just did, what *one* thing can you take action on right now that can improve your financial situation?

_____

Are you really serious about making more money from your real estate? Make a commitment to yourself by signing and dating the following.

I commit to performing the above action steps by _____ (date).

Signature:_____

Today's Date: _____

IF YOU DON'T YET OWN PROPERTY:

1. Why do you want to own real estate? Please list at least three reasons.

1. _____

2. _____

3. _____

(Continued)

(Continued)

2. What three things are stopping you right now from investing in real estate?

    1. _____

    2. _____

    3. _____

3. Now make a commitment to yourself to do the following getting-ready-for-real-estate steps by signing the commitment at the end of the chapter.

    ■ Create a chart of passive appreciation for your hometown over the past five years. Are you above or below the national average? _____

    ■ Determine your ability to get financing. Meet with a mortgage broker (not a loan officer) to review your current creditworthiness.

    ■ Make a list of five things you do really well that could be used to build your real estate fortune.

    _____

    _____

    _____

    _____

    _____

I commit to performing the above action steps by _____ (date).

Signature:_____

Today's Date: _____

Chapter 3

WHAT IT REALLY TAKES TO SUCCEED IN REAL ESTATE

Almost everyone has either owned a house, rented a house, or at the very least lived in a house. It is probably because of this basic familiarity with houses that most people tend to think that they know what's involved in being a real estate investor, as they believe they understand the subject matter, namely houses. Of course, having lived in, rented, or even owned a house does not qualify you as a real estate investor, any more than having enjoyed a glass of wine makes you a vintner. While this may seem obvious, the following is less clear . . .

Most people believe that in order to do well in real estate, they have to study and understand a minimum set of facts, rules, statistics, and strategies. The general belief is that if you read a number of good books on the subject of real estate, or even take a number of courses (and the newspapers are full of advertisements for self-appointed gurus willing to share their secrets with the masses), then you too will be a highly successful and wealthy real estate investor. In theory, this all makes sense: In order to do well in real estate, you have to study and understand relevant information well enough so that you can go out and apply it.

Unfortunately, reality is far removed from this ideal. Dolf and Diane have both observed students who have come to their classes, learned all there is to learn, and still have not managed to become real estate investors. They have also met and heard of countless more who have diligently studied under a number of successful mentors and investors, and who have similarly not made it in real estate. It would seem that it is not sufficient to merely know the facts about real estate investing.

Dolf was so frustrated by his apparent inability to get his real estate message across effectively, that he embarked on an 11-month study to find out why it is that when you give people all they need to know to become fabulously wealthy through real estate, many still do not do it. What he found out astounded him—and completely changed the way he taught real estate.

The first part of his study involved finding out what happens to people who come into money without having to work for it, such as lottery winners. In the United States, when you win the lottery, you do not merely win a few thousand dollars, or even hundreds of thousands of dollars. You win tens of millions of dollars and more—last year four winners shared a

$600 million jackpot. It makes the following fact all the more astounding:

Easy Come, Easy Go

In the United States as in most of the Western World, within five years of winning the lottery, four out of five winners are financially back to where they were before they won the lottery.

In other words, when you give people millions and millions of dollars, 80 percent of the recipients squander the money—divest themselves of it—within five years. This poses a dilemma for teachers like Dolf and Diane. If we know that four out of five people squander money when you give it to them, how can we hope to teach them how to make it *and keep it*? To solve this apparent dilemma, Dolf's 11-month study took him on tangents well away from hard-core real estate, and into the realm of psychology and human nature. This is what he found. . . .

Many of our thoughts and actions are determined by our core beliefs, the subconscious beliefs that have been given to us largely by our parents. Now it is not as if our parents have maliciously set out to undermine our ability to amass wealth. But without knowing it, often our parents gave us beliefs that undermined rather than encouraged us. For instance, as a child you might have asked for a bicycle, and your parent answered, "What do you think, kiddo, that money grows on trees?" The underlying inference here is that money is hard to come by. And if we are told often enough that money is difficult to come by, then we end up believing it. Here are some more beliefs that parents innocently give to their children:

Negative Beliefs About Money

- Money is the root of all evil.
- If you haven't worked hard for money, you don't deserve it.
- You have to have money to make money.
- Money can't buy you happiness.
- It is easier to get a camel through the eye of a needle than for a rich man to get to heaven.

Now we could spend a chapter exploring each of these beliefs. For instance, many people will say that the complete saying regarding money and evil is "For the love of money is the root of all evil." And they would be right. Except that the subconscious mind cannot tell the difference, and simply makes a connection between money and evil.

Think about it: How do we describe the rich? We say they are so rich, they are *filthy* rich! They are so rich, they are *stinking* rich! We associate being rich with filth and stench. So now think back to our innocent lottery winners. Life was fine until they won their tens of millions. Of course initially they were elated with their winnings. But then, as the weeks went by, they suddenly felt evil (or thought their friends might think of them as evil), felt as though they did not deserve it, thought they would no longer be happy, felt they were condemned to hell, and felt filthy and dirty. No wonder they divest themselves of their winnings!

The only way to overcome this subconscious sabotaging of anything good that happens to you financially is to explore the belief systems that are a part of your subconscious, and to set about replacing these limiting beliefs with more empowering ones, beliefs that can help you amass a fortune rather than induce you to divest yourself of the fortune. Such new beliefs may include the following:

Empowering Beliefs About Money

- Money comes easily to me.
- My poverty can help no one, but my wealth can help many people.
- I am a money-making juggernaut.
- Money is good.
- It's fun to help others with my wealth.

The interesting thing about these new beliefs is that you do not even have to believe them yet. So long as you repeat them often enough, preferably every morning and every night, preferably out loud, and preferably in front of someone else (so that your subconscious knows that you are willing to be held accountable), then eventually they will form a part of your subconscious.

The other major finding to come out of Dolf's 11-month study, is that most people have a very dysfunctional relationship with money. When you ask a large group of people in an audience how many have what could be described as a large sum of money on their person, say $1,000 or more, then very few do. And when you ask the masses why they don't have that much on them, you get a vast array of answers, such as "I have credit cards so I don't need cash," or "it's not earning interest in

66

my pocket." However, the bulk of the answers center around three reasons:

> ### Three Reasons for Not Carrying Large Sums of Cash Around
>
> **1.** I may lose it.
> **2.** I may spend it.
> **3.** Someone may steal it.

The first point effectively says that we don't trust ourselves not to lose money, or simply that we don't trust ourselves with money. The second point reinforces this distrust: Even if we don't lose it, we may spend it. (By the way, if you are going to lose it anyway, you may as well spend it first!) Either way, points one and two show that we do not trust ourselves with money. The third point shows that apart from not trusting ourselves with money, we cannot trust other people either, as they may steal it from us.

If we can't trust ourselves, and can't trust others, who is there left to trust? No wonder we are having difficulty amassing a fortune. We cannot even allow ourselves to carry a mere $1,000 in cash around with us. How would we ever cope with $10 million?

So, we recommend that you go to your bank, withdraw $1,000 cash, and carry it around on your person for a month or so. Go on, give it a try. The stranger and scarier it seems to you, perhaps the more you need to do this exercise. But the results could well change your life. People who have tried this report that for perhaps the first time in their lives, they felt as if they were in control of their money.

By the way, we will add a bit of a disclaimer here. Statistically, if a large enough proportion of our readers go out and carry $1,000 around on their person, then some will get mugged. Don't blame us! We are suggesting that carrying this money around on you may benefit your subconscious, but will not be held responsible for any consequences!

DOES THE DEAL OF THE DECADE COME ALONG ABOUT ONCE A WEEK?

Apart from our subconscious beliefs about money, there is another aspect that can help us become great real estate investors, and that is our belief that great deals really exist. If you believe that deals that sound too good to be true are always scams, then you may never be burnt, but you will also never participate in a great deal. Now we are not saying that you should jump in, boots and all, on any deal just because it sounds good. As always, do your due diligence. However, if you eliminate all deals that sound spectacular, then by definition you will limit yourself to mediocre deals, deals that are so lousy that they are likely to be real.

There are 101 reasons why people may sell a piece of real estate at below the market value. If you are open to the possibility that these deals exist, then you will find them. If you think they are all scams, then you will not find them, and your belief that these deals do not exist will be confirmed, at least in your mind.

Zig Ziglar says, "Your attitude determines your altitude." How high do you want to fly when it comes to real estate?

ACTION STEPS

1. Write down the beliefs you were told as a child about money. Set a timer for three minutes and write as many as you can. Remember you may no longer believe these. We are just highlighting how insidious some of these beliefs can be.

2. Write down a new set of beliefs that you would like to think you could believe. You don't even have to believe them right now.

3. Read these new beliefs every morning and every evening, preferably aloud, and preferably in front of someone else. If you keep this up for a month, you will be amazed at how many of these beliefs will become part of your subconscious.

4. Go to the bank and withdraw $1,000 in cash and carry it around for an entire month. If at the end of the month you still feel uncomfortable with this cash on you, then keep carrying it around until it feels like $5 or $10 might feel like today.

5. Write down the two action steps you are prepared to commit to right now.

I commit to performing the above action steps by _____ (date).

Signature:_____

Today's Date: _____

Chapter 4

THE FIVE FUNDAMENTAL WEALTH-BUILDING STRATEGIES OF REAL ESTATE

HOW THE RICH LEGALLY MAKE MORE MONEY

How is it that the rich got that way? Some of them inherited their wealth and some just lucked into it. By and large, though, inheritances and whims of fortune get frittered away. What does it take to create real, sustained wealth that endures through up markets and down markets? What does it take to create the kind of wealth that can create foundations and leave legacies for the future?

It takes doing things differently.

At a young age, Dolf made a study of the wealthy and found that most had either made or held their wealth in real estate. Diane made a similar study of the wealthy clients of her CPA firm. She discovered that the wealthy made purposeful wealth-building decisions based on tax laws. They then used five fundamental wealth-building strategies to exponentially increase their returns from investments. First, though, let's look at the principles of creating tax-advantaged wealth-building strategies.

JUMP START! YOUR WEALTH

Diane introduced the Jump Start! method of tax-advantaged wealth-building in *Loopholes of the Rich—How the Rich Legally Make More Money and Pay Less Tax* (2004, Wiley). (See Figure 4.1.) This method takes advantage of the three major components of favorable tax laws. These are: (1) your business, (2) your real estate investments, and (3) your home. Did you notice that two of the three sources of tax loopholes come from real estate? And, if your business buys the building it is in, you've got yet another real estate component.

There are seven steps to this method. You can choose to do any or all of the following Jump Start! steps. The more fully you participate in as many of the steps as possible, the faster and bigger your positive results will be.

1. *Create a business.* Make sure it's in the proper business structure and that you have anticipated: (1) at least one clear exit strategy, (2) sources of funding for the business, (3) how to take money out of the business, and (4) a strategy to run the business in a way that reduces risk for you. Sometimes starting a business is as simple as changing your employment status from an employee to an independent contractor.
2. *Discover your hidden business deductions.* It can be a major eye-opener when the first-time business owner discovers

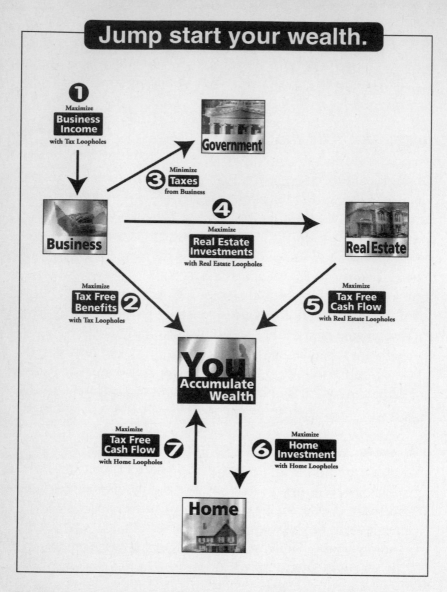

FIGURE 4.1   Jump-start your wealth.

Reprinted with permission from *Loopholes of the Rich*, by Diane Kennedy (Wiley, 2004).

all the things that are now tax-deductible. These are the things you used to spend personal money on. The difference is that they are now deductible. Discover and properly document those expenses. This is how your business can give you money tax free.

3. *Pay your taxes.* Use proper planning to prepay just enough in taxes at the latest possible time. In this way, you can get 0 percent loans from the government on your tax money. When you have multiple businesses in the right structures, you can often select when you want to pay taxes and defer payment to a far-distant time.

4. *What's left goes into real estate.* You might not be able to hit the ideal investment strategy of having all leftover business cash go into real estate. But, the more you can put into real estate, without needing to draw anything for personal living expenses, the faster your income will grow. Make sure your real estate investment is done using the proper leverage with the optimum structures.

5. *Real estate income comes out tax free.* A good real estate investment will create positive cash flow for you. If you have made a good deal, you'll have positive cash flow from the first day. And, if you have a good tax plan, you'll pay *zero taxes* on that cash flow.

6. *Buy a house the right way.* You need a place to live and, let's face it, that's not an asset that will put money in your pocket. In fact, your home quite likely will be one of the biggest expenses you'll have. Look for good deals in neighborhoods that are appreciating and make the best deal possible on financing. Make sure you have a contingency plan in case the value drops and your other income goes down. And, above all, use the homestead laws and/or proper business structures to protect your investment.

7. *Make your home give you money.* The biggest gift that Congress has ever given us is available *only* for homeowners. The one requirement is that you have to move. You can also take the money out, tax free, from your home to invest in other businesses or real estate properties. It's a gift—take advantage of all that the IRS allows.

Did you notice that steps four through seven all relate to real estate? We'll concentrate on those steps throughout the rest of the book. Real estate investing grows wealth even faster when you take advantage of the five wealth-building strategies:

1. Leverage of money.
2. Leverage of time.
3. Velocity.
4. Cash flow.
5. Risk reduction.

WEALTH-BUILDING STRATEGY #1— LEVERAGE OF MONEY

Leverage means to do more with less. It is truly the definition of power. The most obvious leverage comes about from the leverage of money. That's one of the best, most recognizable benefits of real estate—you can use other people's money to build your wealth. Can you do it on your own, paying cash for everything? Of course, but without leverage you've lost some of your power. If you decide to build wealth through real estate and never use the leverage of money, you will need to find another method to create the wealth or resign yourself to the fact that your wealth will grow very slowly.

Imagine having $100,000 to invest in real estate. You choose a slow, safe area to invest in that has experienced an average appreciation of 6 percent per year for the past five years. Your choice is to invest in a building using only cash (your $100,000), or to buy a building for $1,000,000 using financing for 90 percent of the purchase. Now fast forward one year. The two buildings have both appreciated by 6 percent, just as in the past. The $100,000 building is now worth $106,000. The $1,000,000 building is now worth $1,060,000. If you had bought the first building, you would now have equity of $106,000. That's a return of 6 percent. If you had bought the second building, you would now have equity of $160,000. That's a return of 60 percent.

But, wait, you exclaim, "How could I make the payments for the mortgage on the $1,000,000 building? I owe $900,000!" Well, that's where tenants come in. Learn to love tenants because they provide the pathway to wealth. Remember also, if you lose some of the tenants and have periods of negative cash flow, you owe the payments on the building. You won't suddenly owe $900,000. You will owe $7,000 or so each month in payments.

We recommend that you use the Five Basket Method for determining the amount of cash you need for your financial strategies. This method, outlined in our free e-book "Financial Planning for Real Estate Investors" (available at www.DolfAndDiane.com), uses five primary baskets for building your funds:

- Security.
- Emergency.
- Income.
- Growth.
- High-risk.

Security Basket

The Security Basket contains the amount that you put aside in case everything goes wrong—you lose your job and your tenants move out. If you are just beginning, without a lot of investments, a good rule of thumb is to maintain three to six months' worth of expenses in cash in the Security Basket. However, the formula is a little more complicated as you add additional properties. In fact, you can lower your Security Basket needs as your wealth accumulates. For example, the conservative accountant in Diane had always wanted six months' worth of expenses in a very liquid account. However, with over 20 properties, that just became ridiculous. Does it seem reasonable that hundreds of tenants across four states and two countries would suddenly move out all at once?

Emergency Basket

The Emergency Basket covers emergency items that come up just through normal living. It is especially important for people who have experienced credit card debt in the past due to emergencies such as medical issues, car problems, or even the water heater breaking down. The credit card debt comes about because there wasn't an Emergency Basket available to cover the expenses.

Income Basket

The Income Basket is the basket that provides the cash flow to create passive income—the income you don't have to work for. This could also be a business that provides income even when you aren't working or other investments that provide a return of income. In other words, this is the basket that gets you financially free!

Growth Basket

The Growth Basket takes advantage of appreciating markets to build wealth through equity. It could also include other appreciating assets such as a business that at some point could be sold. The easiest way to build the Growth Basket, however, is through the use of real estate.

High-Risk Basket

The High-Risk Basket is for the gambler in us. Use this only after you've built the other four baskets sufficiently to safely build your own wealth. The High-Risk Basket is the source of funds for the investments that have less certain returns. In other words, those are the deals that seem pretty compelling, but down deep we're pretty certain that they are just too good to be true. If you've got all of your other baskets handled, and you want the adrenalin rush of a high-risk investment—use these funds to give yourself a little jolt!

The Power of Leverage of Money

Let's go back to the example of the two houses. Assume that you have followed the "Financial Planning for Real Estate Investors" plan of baskets. You've got the risk covered. Knowing that, would you rather have $60,000 or $6,000 after just one year of investing? The power of leverage gives you the bigger return.

Financial Planning for Real Estate Investors

Make sure you have sufficient funds in each of the following baskets:

Security. With no property, consider 3–6 months of expenses. Decrease if you have multiple sources of income.

Emergency. Make sure you have enough to cover emergencies. A good rule of thumb is $2,000 to $5,000 plus $1,000 per each family member.

Income. Invest enough so that you have passive income to provide for all of your expenses. The amount needed will vary based on the return from your assets.

Growth. This fund protects against inflation and currency fluctuation. The exact amount will be a factor based on the worldwide diversification of your investments and the return of capital.

High-Risk. This fund provides the "roll the dice" funds for high-risk ventures. It's not necessary to put money aside if your personality type is not such that this is appealing. But if you're always excited by the next get-rich-quick scheme, then give yourself a budget for those ventures and stick to it. Otherwise, use the tried-and-true methods to build your wealth.

WEALTH BUILDING STRATEGY #2— LEVERAGE OF TIME

Why do you want to invest in real estate? Most people are looking to build real estate wealth because they think that those sources of income will give them more freedom. That freedom is usually expressed as the freedoms of choice, flexibility, and primarily time. Yet, these same people who are looking for more time through real estate sometimes end up spending all of their time finding, fixing up, managing, and selling real estate. What went wrong?

The problem is that they haven't fully understood and used the leverage of time that is also available for real estate investors. The easiest way to think about this form of leverage is to picture a simple lever. It's nothing more than a long board resting on a fulcrum. On one side of the lever, picture all the things you want from real estate. A sample of those benefits might be: choice, time, money, passive income, wealth, and retirement. The fulcrum that moves those things is your real estate investments (Figure 4.2). The five forces that move that lever are:

1. Knowledge.
2. Systems.
3. Other people's time.
4. Other people's knowledge.
5. Other people's systems.

Knowledge

Notice that knowledge is closest to the middle. Have you ever noticed that as you move out on the lever, you need to apply

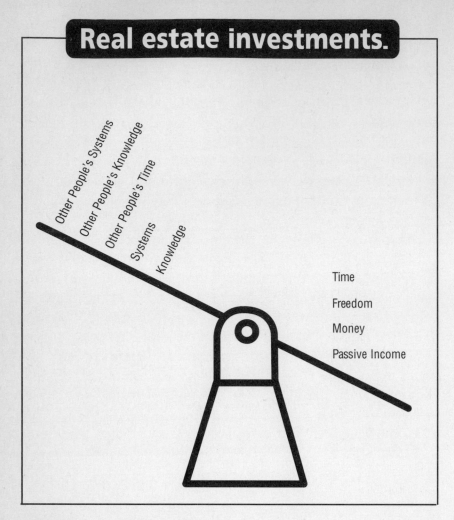

FIGURE 4.2   Real estate investments.

less and less pressure to make the other side move? The leverage points closer to the fulcrum have less power available.

The knowledge you gain by yourself is a critical first step, but it is also the least powerful leverage point. This is the knowledge you gain about finding, investing, fixing, maintaining, and leasing real estate, and knowledge you personally gain about running a business. At this level, though, it's just you getting the knowledge. You have to put more effort into it, because you have to do all the work as well. That's why it seems hard to find the time for your investments in the beginning.

Systems

The second point, moving out away from the fulcrum, is systems. These are the systems that you develop in defining how things get done for your company. At this point, you're still doing all of the work. In the beginning with your business, this might be the way you feel you need to operate due to cash flow concerns. You might even decide to handle your accounting and tax work yourself during this step. The systems make it easier, but it still is a lot of work because you have to do it all.

Other People's Time

The third point is other people's time. You hire advisors and employees to help you by adding their expertise. You're now also starting to see more leverage from your actions. That's because other people are doing work. You don't need to do everything; you have other people working with you. By the way, you don't need to spend a certain amount of time or own a certain number of properties until you get to this point. We have a whole section near the end of the book on how to develop your team.

For many people, this is as far as they can see how to use leverage in their business. And, to be honest, we've seen people only get this far and make over a million dollars a year. They mastered the first three leverage points: knowledge, systems, and other people's time. But there are two more leverage points, even more powerful than the others, still available!

Other People's Knowledge

The fourth point is other people's knowledge. This is the point that many people get stuck on. They want to be the smartest person they know and even though they may claim otherwise, they get rid of anyone who might challenge their authority or their ideas. It's the old "my way or the highway" management style.

A powerful way to use other people's knowledge is by hiring the best advisors. Do your current advisors know more than you do? Or, does it feel like you're constantly giving them new ideas to research?

You'll know you're fully immersed in using other people's knowledge, as well as the first three leverage points, when you sometimes feel that you're not familiar with all the details, but you do know that all of your statistics are going up. There is money in your bank. Your wealth is increasing. Your personal baskets are all filling up nicely.

Other People's Systems

The fifth leverage point is even more significant. It's other people's systems. Have you ever found a brilliant advisor and had a great relationship at first, only to have him get so busy he couldn't return your phone calls anymore? You can find people who have the knowledge, if you're lucky, but it's very rare to find top advisors who also know how to build businesses themselves. Other people's systems means that you have others on your team who can deliver high-quality, consistent advice to their clients, no matter how many clients they have. Systems allow quality leverage to occur. With all five leverage points, you are maximizing your leverage plus other people's leverage. The bottom line is that you'll get more powerful results more rapidly.

Five Points of Leverage— The Secret of Creating More Time

1. *Knowledge.* Build your knowledge of your business and all of its components.
2. *Systems.* Develop systems for repetitive tasks and activities.
3. *Other people's time.* You don't have to do it to get it done.
4. *Other people's knowledge.* Hire advisors who have information that enhances your projects. Don't be the smartest, most capable person on your team.
5. *Other people's systems.* Work with outside contractors who have systems of their own. You should never have to worry about whether one of your team members will have time to return your phone call.

WEALTH-BUILDING FACTOR #3—VELOCITY

Many wealth planners talk about the need to assess your current financial status and then determine where you want to be in order to create the plan for building wealth. We definitely agree that is important. But, we want to talk about an additional component—velocity. Velocity is the speed at which you're moving on that path. Once you've calculated your velocity, you'll not only know where you are going but how fast it will take to get there.

First, though, let's investigate the source of the term *velocity*. Macroeconomics, the study of broad economic activities and trends, is possibly the largest subfield in economics. And, it's from economics classes that the term *velocity* in relationship to money was first used. The velocity of money refers to the number of times an individual unit of currency turns over (e.g., is spent) in a specific period of time. Velocity affects the amount of economic activity generated by a given money supply. Velocity is important for measuring the rate at which money in circulation is used for purchasing goods and services. This helps investors gauge how robust the economy is. The faster the velocity is, the stronger the economy will be.

The same is true for your own "economy" or the amount of wealth you have. The faster your personal decision-making and decision-acting velocity, the more wealth you will create. Some of the components of velocity are your abilities to:

- Make a quick go/no go decision.
- Act on decisions to improve the value of your property.
- Keep your money working for you through maximum leverage.

Earlier we discussed how the leverage of money works to build you wealth faster. Now, let's look at that same example and add the velocity to the leverage of money (Figure 4.3).

Plan A Twenty Years, Buy and Wait

House   10%—$20,000   5% Appreciation

$200,000 house   **New Equity—$427,519**

Plan B Twenty Years, Buy and Use Leverage

House   10%—$20,000   5% Appreciation

$200,000 house

In 5 years

In 5 more years

In 5 more years

In 5 more years

New Equity—$6,780,362

FIGURE 4.3   Leverage of money.

In the first plan, let's assume that you buy a property for $200,000 with 10 percent down. We'll assume that your property only goes up in value by 5 percent and that you rent the property for the exact amount of costs. That means no cash flow in or out—it's neutral. At the end of 20 years, your $20,000 equity has become $427,519.

In the second plan, let's assume that you buy the same property with 10 percent down. Only in this case, you refinance in five years to take the equity out of the property. You use that money to buy another property with 10 percent. You wait five years and repeat. At the end of 20 years, your $20,000 equity has now become $6,780,362.

The difference between those two plans is millions of dollars and yet no extra money was used to create the extra value. Velocity made the difference.

Potential Velocity Trap

Contingent liability can reduce your velocity. This includes personal guarantees, co-signing for loans, or acting as a co-borrower. You might sign, without thinking, for a loan for a friend or perhaps your child, and then find years later that this loan actually counts against your borrowing capacity. In other words, the co-signing hurt your personal velocity ability. Think before you sign!

WEALTH-BUILDING STRATEGY #4—CASH FLOW

"Cash is king" is the old saying. Positive cash flow is what keeps your investing going. In fact, one of the baskets of cash is income from passive investments. You can't fill that basket with assets unless those assets create cash flow.

We frequently meet people who have a "great" deal on a vacation property or on bare land. They believe that any real estate is good real estate and so forget about why they're investing in real estate in the first place. If your goal for real estate is to create alternative sources of income, then be very careful where you invest. Fill up your "income" basket first before you move to "high-risk."

Above all, keep the cash flow going so you have the cash you need to keep your whole plan working. It is possible to find properties that create positive cash flow. They might not be readily available in your home town and that's when you will need to look for more creative deals or possibly look outside your home.

One of Diane's clients is a real estate broker who was nervously moving back into real estate after a series of financial disasters in the early 1990s. Back then, she had owned 10 single-family homes with negative cash flow. She didn't worry that she needed to keep putting money into the properties to just make the monthly payments because they were all greatly appreciating. This was during the 1980s in Phoenix, Arizona. Then, the real estate market downturn struck. The properties suddenly weren't worth as much. Plus, she worked in real estate and that industry was really down, so she was facing much lower income from her job.

She was now in a bind. She couldn't afford to keep paying for those negative cash flowing properties and the market was down. She panicked and sold them for even greater losses. When it was all done, she barely was able to avoid bankruptcy. Now she looked again at building a real estate portfolio. But this time she wanted to do it in a smart way by taking advantage of the five fundamental wealth-building strategies. Key for her was to make sure that the properties all created cash flow and created passive income. Will she make it? It's hard to say. She has to overcome the big emotional loss first before she ever fully trusts the real estate market again.

Make sure your real estate investments can weather down markets by ensuring there is always good cash flow.

WEALTH-BUILDING STRATEGY #5— RISK REDUCTION

There's no sense building wealth if you aren't also building a plan on how you're going to keep it. There are two main risks that you'll face as you build your real estate empire: risk from lawsuits and risk from excess tax.

Early on we explained how much easier it was to build wealth using real estate than it was to build wealth using stocks. But, there is one inherent risk to real estate that stocks do not have. We call them tenants! Real estate is a real, tangible, physical proof of an asset. And there are semistrangers in contact with this asset every single day. You need to protect yourself and the property against frivolous lawsuits. Additionally, you might have a situation where you are personally sued. For example, let's say you are a doctor and are suddenly personally sued for something related to your practice. You need to protect your assets against claims that might come about because of your personal acts.

There are three ways to protect your real estate assets:

1. Insurance.
2. Debt.
3. Business structure.

Insurance

Property insurance protects the value of the property against certain hazards. Notice that we said "certain" hazards. There are many catastrophic events that can be excluded from a traditional policy such as earthquakes and hurricanes. These so-called "Acts of God" will require supplemental insurance policies.

Insurance generally has insufficient limits to protect you in case of a lawsuit. In our lawsuit-happy culture, this is becoming a growing problem for real estate owners. If someone slips and falls and a jury determines that you, as landlord, were negligent in some way, you might get hit with a huge judgment. With a judgment in hand, the litigant (the person who sued you) can take your apartment building, your other property, and even your personal residence.

The first level of defense is to make sure you have adequate insurance. Consider getting an "umbrella insurance policy" to cover higher limits of liability. This is a policy that is usually linked to your personal residence. The cost generally ranges about $500 to $1,000 per year for $1,000,000 of liability protection. Is that enough? It's hard to say. If you are sued for less than that, you're fine. But, if something bad really does happen and your property is somehow found to be involved by a jury, then $1,000,000 probably won't be enough.

Debt

You've probably heard the popular advice to pay off your mortgages early so that you can have your properties free and clear. Maybe you've thought of that as well, as a way of reducing your risk for the property. But the fact is that you actually reduce risk when you have debt, not when you pay it off.

Let's use an example of someone who has a home with a $150,000 mortgage. The house is currently worth $180,000, so there is $30,000 worth of equity. But, our homeowner is worried about losing his job and so he makes the decision to start paying extra money on the note. Each month he pays an extra $1,000 toward the note balance. The mortgage balance keeps going down as his equity grows. And then, a few years later, the thing he feared most happens—he loses his job! But, he thinks, I'm safer now because I have paid extra on my note balance. Imagine his shock when he discovers that the bank still expects the regular payment next month. It doesn't matter that he has paid an extra $30,000 into the house. In fact, the bank is just all the more pleased when they foreclose on the property. You see the extra payments didn't protect the homeowner, they protected the bank!

If he had completely paid the house off and had it free and clear, he would lose the risk from foreclosure, but he would be even more of a target for lawsuits. Plus, he would have lost the wealth-building strategy of leverage of money.

Seen in this light, debt actually protects the property owner.

Business Structure

The most popular way to protect property is through a properly set up and maintained business structure. There are four good business structures that can be used to own real estate. Selecting the best structure for your investments will depend on where the property is located and what you intend to do with the property.

Generally, if you are buying a property to flip, you will have earned income. Earned income is money you work for. This income is subject to a self-employment tax of 15.3 percent if you hold the property in your own name, in the name of an LLC taxed at the default of single-member status, or partnership or if the property is held in the name of a general partnership. If the property is held in your own name, you have extra tax due to the self-employment tax plus you put all of your other property at risk. The same risk occurs if the property is in the name of a general partnership. An LLC will give you asset protection, but if you are the only owner (called a single member) and you do not elect to be taxed as an S corporation or C corporation, you will have self-employment tax. If you have an LLC with multiple owners (called a multimember LLC) and have not elected to be taxed as an S corporation or a C corporation, you will again have self-employment tax. Remember, though, there is self-employment tax only when you have earned income.

If you are buying property to hold, the income you earn is considered passive income. The best business structures for passive income properties are either the LLC with the default taxation structure or a limited partnership (LP).

Basics of Business Structures for Real Estate Investors

- Know your exit strategy for the property.
- If plan is to flip property, use an S corporation or a C corporation.
- If plan is to hold the property, use an LLC or an LP.

Risk from Excess Tax

It's amazing how many people we run into who are afraid to make more money because they don't want to pay more tax. If you want to pay less tax, the secret is not how much money you make, it's how you make your money. The government provides tax loopholes for real estate investors as an incentive to promote investments. We've discussed some of the tax benefits of real estate in previous chapters.

A significant part of a good real estate investing strategy is minimizing risk from lawsuits and from excess tax. In both cases, you need experienced advisors and a well-thought-out plan to make sure you are taking advantage of all possible advantages.

> ### Maximize the Five Fundamental
> ### Wealth-Building Strategies of Real Estate
>
> 1. *Leverage of money.* Use other people's money to build your wealth.
> 2. *Leverage of time.* Use your knowledge and systems to maximize other people's time, knowledge, and systems.
> 3. *Velocity.* Get your program set and then move forward with confidence.
> 4. *Cash flow.* Always remember the fundamental—get the money!
> 5. *Risk reduction.* Protect what you build.

ACTION STEPS

1. Goal: Improve Your Leverage of Money

   a. Review your current debt.

   b. How much total do you owe in debt that does not build assets? (Bad Debt)

     $_____

   c. How much total do you owe in debt that does build assets? (Good Debt)

     $_____

   d. What percentage do you have in bad debt? (Bad Debt/ (Good Debt + Bad Debt))

   _____

   e. If you have bad debt now, what three things can you do within the next week to reduce the amount of bad debt you have?

     1. _____

     2. _____

     3. _____

   f. Review the five baskets of cash: emergency, security, income, growth, and high-risk at www.DolfAndDiane.com.

   g. What are three things you can do within the next month to begin growing your own baskets of income?

     1. _____

     2. _____

     3. _____

(Continued)

(Continued)

h. If you don't have good debt, what are three things you can do *within the next week* to increase the amount of good debt that you have?

1. _____

2. _____

3. _____

2. Goal: Improve Your Leverage of Time
Review each of the five leverage points to create more time:

a. Knowledge
Do you need more knowledge in investing, financing, accounting or tax? What are three things you can do to gain the knowledge you need?

1. _____

2. _____

3. _____

b. Systems
Do you have established systems for buying, holding, selling, improving, and renting your property and handling the accounting and tax needs? What systems do you want to create or improve?

1. _____

2. _____

3. _____

c. Other People's Time

Are you doing only the things that you love to do and that you do well? If not, what three things would you love to turn over to someone knowing that they could do it better than you do?

1. _____

2. _____

3. _____

d. Other People's Knowledge

How smart are your advisors? Are they bringing you info? Or, are you bringing ideas to them? What three areas do you want your advisors to know better than you do?

1. _____

2. _____

3. _____

e. Other People's Systems

If you have people on your team now, are they ready for growth? What happens if someone on your team is out of town or has a sudden emergency? If you're ready for change, what are two things you can do to start that process?

1. _____

2. _____

3. _____

(Continued)

(Continued)

3. Goal: Improve Your Velocity
   What are three things you can do to improve the rate of speed at which you're growing your wealth?

   1. _____
   2. _____
   3. _____

4. Goal: Improve Your Cash Flow
   Are your expenses currently covered by the cash flow from your properties? If not, what are three things you can immediately do to improve your cash flow?

   1. _____
   2. _____
   3. _____

5. Goal: Reduce Risk for Your Assets

   a. What asset protection plan are you currently using to protect your real estate?

   _____

   b. How much equity do you currently have at risk in your investments?
   $ _____

   c. How can you use the risk reduction techniques of insurance, debt, and business structures with your current investments?

   _____

6. Review
What three action steps from above are the highest priority for you to act on right now?

1. _____

2. _____

3. _____

I commit to performing the above action steps by _____
(date).

Signature:_____

Today's Date: _____

Chapter 5

WHAT TYPE OF INVESTOR ARE YOU?

WHAT DO *YOU* WANT FROM REAL ESTATE?

In the past few chapters, we've shared some of our personal investing stories as well as results that our clients have had from their real estate investing. Did you notice how the reasons for getting involved in real estate were all as varied as the people themselves?

Some of the reasons that we've heard for investing in real estate are:

Quick cash.

Cash flow.

Replace other income.

Hold wealth (something to do while they're making other income).

Replace lost wealth from the stock market.

Create wealth.

Replace a job.

Create retirement.

Freedom.

What do you want from real estate? One of the biggest challenges we've seen from investors comes from the sheer amount of opportunity that they see as they start investigating. Some are intrigued by the possibility to make quick cash through flipping, or quick selling, property. Others want to create replacement income so they can leave their job. Oh, and there is an area over here that could be developed into a different land use. And, what about those appreciation rates over in California? There are just too many opportunities.

> *The problem is not lack of opportunity.*
> *The problem is choking on opportunity.*

Be clear at the outset of what your goal is as you invest in real estate. What is it you want from your investments? And then develop a plan to give you that. Learn to say "no" to deals that don't fit the outcome you want. They can be great ways to make money . . . for someone else. If it's not fulfilling what you want, it's just a distraction from your purpose.

INVESTOR IQ

Added to the challenge of deciding why you want real estate, and the form of investing you want to do, is the responsibility of self-assessment. In Chapter 3, we discussed what it really takes to succeed in real estate from a mindset perspective. Now let's look at your skills. In this case, however, it's not a question of how fast you can operate a calculator or paint a wall. It's a question of how capable you are at leveraging your time and money as you manage your velocity.

In the following test, you will be asked questions that will assess your ability to leverage money. Wherever you find you are after taking the test, you will see that there is a form of investing that will work with you. If you'd like to move up the scale, we'll also give you some exercises that can help you do that.

First, the person who has a lower-number score on the test is opposed to the leverage of money. He wants to pay cash and has a high need for security. A person who has a higher-number score fully utilizes (or is ready to utilize) the leverage of money. She understands and uses good debt to build assets. The difference isn't an acceptance of risk as much as it is an ability to fully fund the baskets of income to reduce risk as you add debt that builds your assets. These five baskets are:

1. Security.
2. Emergency.
3. Cash flow.
4. Growth.
5. High risk.

The second metric that is measured is your ability to leverage time. In other words, how easy is it for you to increase your knowledge, create systems, and use other people's time, knowledge, and systems? A person with a low score for the leverage of time generally wants to learn by doing and wants to fully understand what is going on with an investment first. This can be an effective way to learn and it's not uncommon for investors to start off with an opposing leverage of time ability to end up with an embracing leverage of time ability. At the opposite end of the scale an investor is generally in a position where she just reviews financial data on a property and doesn't need to be involved in the day-to-day management.

The third metric is velocity. Velocity refers to how fast you can move your money and your ideas and the rate of speed at which you make and act on a decision. The measure of velocity is based on your level of leverage of time and leverage of money. The higher your ability is to leverage time and money, the faster your velocity. In this case, the scale of velocity ranges from 1 to 9. It is a relative scale, with the velocity of 1 meaning that you do not use debt (leverage of money) and have a need to "do it yourself." Your wealth can grow, but at a slower pace than a person who has a velocity of 9, which means that you fully utilize the leverage of money and time. Your velocity measurement is your Investor IQ.

Leverage of Money Test

1. When it comes to credit cards, I:
   a. Don't use credit cards.
   b. Use credit cards and pay off the balance each month.
   c. Have too much debt.

2. I feel secure when I:
   a. Have no debt.
   b. Have passive income that greatly exceeds my normal expenses.
   c. Have paid off my home.

3. The bank calls you and tells you that you are eligible for a home equity loan on your house; you:

    a. Ask how much the rate is.

    b. Politely decline.

    c. Ask if it is possible to refinance the entire balance and pull some cash out.

4. You own real estate investment property in an area that is appreciating; you:

    a. Refinance to pull out equity and buy additional property.

    b. Are really happy with the increasing equity.

    c. Consider buying more property.

5. You own your own residence, and discover that you could pay your house off in just nine years by making extra payments of less than $500 per month; you:

    a. Begin immediately paying extra off of your home.

    b. Analyze what the benefit would really be to pay off the house.

    c. Are too busy to read the offer from the mortgage company.

6. The safest place to keep your money is:

    a. In your home or other properties, held in proper business structures.

    b. In the mattress.

    c. In liquid accounts in your own name.

7. You would consider refinancing a property to pull out cash if:

    a. You knew with 100 percent certainty you would not put your house at risk.

    b. You knew what you would do with the money.

    c. You'd never do it.

8. Regarding the five baskets of money: security, emergency, income, growth, and high risk, you:

    a. Have fully funded all baskets.

    b. Have begun a plan to begin funding the baskets.

    c. Don't remember what that meant.

9. You currently have:

    a. High credit card debt.

    b. Mortgages on your properties that give you cash flow.

    c. Mortgages only on your home and/or vacation home.

10. Debt makes you:

    a. Scared.

    b. Plan heavily.

    c. Happy.

Remember there are no right or wrong answers as you grade your test. This is simply a way of determining what your current views on leverage of money are and how that will impact the velocity of your wealth-building.

Grading the Leverage of Money Test

Question 1:   a = 2, b = 3, c = 1

Question 2:   a = 1, b = 3, c = 2

Question 3:   a = 3, b = 1, c = 3

Question 4:   a = 3, b = 1, c = 2

Question 5:   a = 1, b = 3, c = 2

Question 6:   a = 3, b = 1, c = 1

Question 7:   a = 2, b = 3, c = 1

Question 8:   a = 3, b = 2, c = 1

Question 9:   a = 1, b = 3, c = 1

Question 10:   a = 1, b = 2, c = 3

If your total is:

10–15	Current Leverage of Money is:	Low (1)
16–22	Current Leverage of Money is:	Medium (2)
23–30	Current Leverage of Money is:	High (3)

Leverage of Time Test

1. Hours you spend monthly on your financial education:
   a. 0–2 hours.
   b. 2–10 hours.
   c. 10+ hours.

2. Likelihood that you will implement an action plan from an idea you read:
   a. I jump right in and figure it out later.
   b. As soon as I understand everything about it, I'll act.

c. If I understand the concept, I'll take some form of action within the next week.

3. A system is defined as something that you could give to a reasonably skilled person and, after one day or less of instruction, could then turn the task over to him. How many systems have you created and implemented in your own business or real estate investing?

   a. 0.
   b. 1–2.
   c. More than 2.

4. How much of your work time do you spend on things that you truly love and that give you energy?

   a. 0–10%.
   b. 11–30%.
   c. 31%+.

5. What is your first thought when someone suggests adding an expert to your team?

   a. I already have a great team!
   b. I can't find anyone smarter than me.
   c. It's too expensive.

6. My biggest problem with my tax advisor is:

   a. He/she is too expensive.
   b. I can't keep up with all of his/her great ideas.
   c. I'm afraid I'll outgrow him/her (or I'm afraid I already have).

7. I regularly work with a real estate agent to find property:

  a. Rarely.
  b. Occasionally.
  c. Frequently.

8. The best deal I've ever done in real estate:

  a. Is still out there.
  b. Was within the last year.
  c. Was over 5 years ago.

9. I spend most of my time on:

  a. Negotiation and setting up property deals.
  b. Administrative functions for my business.
  c. Getting ready to start investing in real estate.

10. The best way for me to work with my advisors is:

  a. In face-to-face meetings.
  b. Consistently via phone, fax, or e-mail in proactive plans.
  c. When I need immediate advice.

Grading the Leverage of Time Test

Question 1:   a = 2, b = 3, c = 1

Question 2:   a = 1, b = 3, c = 2

Question 3:   a = 3, b = 1, c = 3

Question 4:   a = 3, b = 1, c = 2

Question 5:   a = 1, b = 3, c = 2

Question 6:   a = 3, b = 1, c = 1

Question 7:   a = 2, b = 3, c = 1

Question 8:   a = 3, b = 2, c = 1

Question 9:   a = 1, b = 3, c = 1

Question 10:   a = 1, b = 2, c = 3

If your total is:

10–15	Current Leverage of Money is:	Low (1)
16–22	Current Leverage of Money is:	Medium (2)
23–30	Current Leverage of Money is:	High (3)

What's Your Velocity?

Now multiply the leverage of time factor by the leverage of money factor. Your answer will be somewhere between 1 and 9. The fastest velocity is 9; the slowest is 1. As you begin investing in real estate, it's often best to start with a slow velocity. You might want to ensure cash flow by putting more money down and by being very careful with your other sources of debt or income. Additionally, it might be a good idea to also do many of the tasks of renovating and leasing your property in the beginning. This will give you experience that will be helpful as you develop systems and begin working with professionals.

But if you have a low velocity and you're not a brand-new investor, consider pushing outside your box a little. The higher the velocity, the more potential wealth you can create for yourself, your family, and your community.

ACTION STEPS

1. Take the test in this chapter.
2. Are you satisfied with the results? Is this the right place for you to be in your real estate career?
3. If you're ready for a change in the speed in which you grow wealth, what two actions can you take right now to increase your velocity?

   1. _____

   2. _____

4. For additional tips go to www.DolfAndDiane.com. What action steps can you take after reviewing the new ideas posted there?

   _____

5. What two actions steps do you want to take as a result of reviewing the above?

   1. _____

   2. _____

   I commit to performing the above action steps by _____ (date).

   Signature:_____

   Today's Date: _____

PART TWO

Getting Ready for Real Estate

Chapter 6

CATEGORIES OF REAL ESTATE

Most people, when they think of real estate, think in terms of either residential real estate or commercial real estate. What's more, when given the choice of investing in either of these two categories, most people prefer residential real estate for the simple reason that they are reasonably familiar with residential property (almost everyone has lived in a house!). Therefore, they have a reasonable idea as to what they are looking for if they are looking to invest. For instance, even the most naïve investors would know that a house must have a kitchen, a front door, and a roof, to attract even the most disinterested tenant. However, when it comes to commercial property, many people are so unfamiliar with what a tenant could reasonably expect, that they shy away from commercial real estate altogether.

In this chapter we are going to compare residential real estate with commercial real estate, and discover many other categories of real estate that are equally valid.

RESIDENTIAL REAL ESTATE

As we have already observed, most people, when they think about investing in real estate, think in terms of investing in *residential* real estate. Given that most people (with the exception of park-bench dwellers and a handful of people institutionalized for whatever reason) live in a residence of one form or another, then this habit of focusing on residential property is totally understandable. In fact, when you add up the total value of all residential properties in the United States, that value exceeds all the capital tied up in all other industries combined, and yet few economists acknowledge real estate as being the biggest industry in the country.

Clearly, investing in residential real estate as opposed to any other category of real estate has some advantages. First, houses are everywhere, so you do not have to go far to find potential deals. Second, with the typical American moving on average every five years, and millions of citizens being born and dying every year, there is a constant stream of supply and demand, making real estate not only the most capital intensive, but also one of the most vibrant industries there is. Third, since everyone is so familiar with what is involved in living in a house, you do not need to learn much to be a residential property landlord.

Having acknowledged these advantages, however, we are astounded at how many investors never move on from residential real estate. Our surprise comes about because despite the advantages of residential real estate mentioned above, there are so many great advantages of commercial real estate that once they have tried commercial real estate, many serious investors never go back to residential.

In his book *Real Estate Riches* (Wiley, 2004), Dolf devotes a chapter to comparing residential real estate with commercial real estate. We won't repeat all the information here, but will highlight some of the main points.

Residential real estate is, by definition, real estate that occupants use as their residence. Thus, even though for mortgage purposes a multiplex with more than four units is considered commercial (and so attracts commercial interest rates and fees), since it is still providing residential accommodation, we will categorize it as residential. After all, you still have to deal with residential tenants (a lot of them) in a 98-plex!

Similarly, commercial real estate is, by definition, any real estate where commerce is carried out. Hence, it includes shops, strip malls, office buildings, oil refineries, restaurants, storage units, automotive assembly plants, plant nurseries, motels, bicycle repair shops, hairdressing salons, warehouses, factories, hotels, convention centers, call centers, telephone exchanges, lumber yards, veterinary surgeries, funeral parlors, and ice-cream stores.

One of the most fundamental differences between residential and commercial real estate, which you must understand to embark on a foray into commercial investing, is that with residential real estate you are essentially dealing with people, whereas with commercial real estate you are essentially dealing with contracts.

Now we know that you could argue that commercial real estate involves people as well (the person you negotiate with, who signs your lease, pays the rent, etc.) and that residential real estate involves contracts as well (the residential tenancy agreement, for instance). However, realistically, with residential real estate it boils down to your opinion versus that of the tenant. For instance, your tenancy agreement may well state that the property shall be kept in a clean and tidy condition, but your views on what constitutes cleanliness and tidiness may well differ from that of your tenant, and then you have, potentially, a dispute on your hands. You have to deal with people! Conversely, a commercial lease agreement that stipulates how a property shall be kept is usually backed up by clauses that state that if the property is not maintained in the prescribed manner, then the landlord shall have the right to send in cleaning crews *and send the bill to the tenant.* You are now dealing with contracts.

Once you understand the fundamental difference between dealing with tenants versus contracts, then all the other advantages of commercial real estate fall into place. They can be summarized as follows:

1. Commercial tenants sign up on long-term contracts (leases) varying in duration from 2 years for a simple shop, to 25 years or more for well-located office space, whereas most residential tenancies are typically month-by-month, sometimes for six months or a year at a time, and rarely for longer. In other words, you have greater peace of mind and more stable rentals from commercial.

2. The government tends not to interfere with contracts freely entered into by commercial landlords and tenants, whereas in most countries governments actively support the perceived underdog (the tenant!) against the rapacious claws of racketeering residential landlords. While their intentions are no doubt good, we cannot understand why tenants who have signed an agreement to pay rent by

a certain date should be given up to 45 days' grace (as they are in California, for instance) before the landlord can even begin to take remedial action. If that same tenant filled up with gas and took off without paying, the authorities would be after him with flashing lights, but it seems acceptable in our society for residential tenants not to pay their rent. Unfortunately, many tenants take advantage of this government-sanctioned grace period!

3. Commercial tenants tend to earn their income from their premises. Often, their own clients come to the premises. Hence, the tenants have a vested interest in keeping the property looking good. We constantly get requests from our commercial tenants (as required by the lease agreement) to renovate, modernize, or otherwise improve our buildings at their expense, something that has never happened with our residential properties.

4. Commercial tenants tend to pay for all outgoings associated with their tenancy, such as property taxes, insurance, and maintenance of all aspects of the property apart from the exterior water-tightness. With residential real estate, the burden of paying these expenses falls on the landlord, thereby eroding the returns.

5. If you want to own $300,000 worth of real estate, then one or two houses could let you reach your quota. However, if you want to own $10 million of real estate, then you will end up owning a lot of residential real estate, with a lot of bathrooms, kitchens, and lavatories to maintain. The management burden would be substantial, even if you employed property managers to do the work for you. However, $10 million of commercial real estate could comprise one or two buildings, with commensurately much less management overhead. Commercial is simpler.

These points highlight just some of the advantages of commercial real estate over residential real estate. However, there are also two disadvantages that we should look at.

First, the proportion of the purchase price that a bank will lend on a commercial property (the loan-to-value ratio) is typically less than what they will lend on a residential property. While 90 percent may be common on residential, 60 percent is more typical for commercial real estate.

Second, if your residential property is vacant, then generally you have to do only one thing to fill it: Drop the rent. However, if your commercial property is vacant, then dropping the rent may not attract a tenant at all, as the property may be unsuited to most commercial uses (it is difficult to sell shoes from a restaurant premise, or to prepare food and serve diners in a motel, or to accommodate people in a fuel depot, or to store fuel in a shoe shop). Hence, even though you tend to have long-term leases, when you do get a vacancy, it can last a lot longer than with residential property.

Having summarized the differences between residential and commercial real estate, let's now look at the various categories of commercial real estate that you can get into.

- *Office space.* Many real estate empires have been built on office space alone. A large office building may have retail tenants on the ground floor, and parking space for more than the workers in the offices, but the bulk of the income comes from long-term leases on office space.
- *Retail.* Entire shopping malls are based on this category of commercial real estate alone, but retail includes small, standalone shops, strip malls, shopping plazas, underground shops by metro stations, and more.

- *Industrial.* Factories, assembly plants, petrochemical facilities, oil refineries, engine reconditioning centers, and aircraft maintenance hangers can all be considered industrial real estate. The list seems endless!
- *Hospitality.* This category includes restaurants, coffee shops, hotels, motels, youth hostels, backpackers' hostels, tourist adventure facilities, and visitor information kiosks.
- *Specialist.* Dolf and Diane have, between them, a veterinary surgery, a funeral parlor, a boat storage facility, an ambulance depot, and an outpatients' operating theater. Some properties just don't fit naturally into any particular category!
- *Leasehold.* Most people think that in order to own a property, you must own the underlying land. This is not always the case. If you own the land and buildings, then you own the property in "fee simple." However, ownership of the land can be separated from ownership of the buildings. If you are the building owner, then you may simply lease the land from the land owner. In this case, you own the leasehold of the property. There is nothing wrong with not owning the land. In fact, since you cannot depreciate land, it makes perfect tax sense to buy leasehold property: You don't need to spend money on the one thing that you cannot depreciate, the rental on the land is tax-deductible, and if the rent gets reviewed only every seven years, then you have six out of seven years where the rental is below market.
- *No land at all.* Even with leasehold land, however, there is still land under your buildings. But who is to say that real estate requires there to be any land at all? One of us owns several marine farms out at sea—the geographic location of the farms is delineated, and the farm is leased from the

government for up to 35 years. Sometimes you have to think and act laterally.

- *Mineral rights.* Another form of not owning any land comes from mineral rights. In some places (in the United States notably Texas and Oklahoma) it is possible to sell land *but retain the mineral rights.* This means that the mineral rights holder owns any minerals such as precious metals or petroleum products under the land. The holder of these rights can drill exploratory bores and effect the extraction of these minerals. One of us owns oil rights but no land. Surely this is still a real estate deal?

- *Air space.* If you thought we were stretching credibility by stating you could own real estate without there being any land to speak of, then you must think we are really stretching the truth by claiming that you can own nothing but the air *above* an existing building on an existing piece of land. And yet this is not only possible, it is very common in commercial real estate, especially with office towers. For instance, a major department store may own the existing two floors of a building, but have no desire to add more stories as they know that their clients do not like going up more than one flight. There is nothing to stop them selling the air rights, or everything above their two floors. A developer or end user may then build on top of the two floors to create office space. In fact, often a high price is paid for air rights (nothing but thin air, remember) with no intent of ever building in that air space—they are paying for the thin air to be kept as just that, thin air. Why? They own the residential tower next door, and want to ensure that their beautiful views of the harbor or mountains or whatever remain unobstructed.

It is possible for a property to fall into several categories simultaneously. For instance, a building may have retail shops on the ground floor and offices above. A campground may incorporate a convenience store and gas station. Some large towers even have hotel rooms, residences, offices, shops, parking, restaurants, and a helipad. Often, the presence of one category can strengthen the viability of the others. We have just delineated these broad categories here to make you realize there are more kinds of real estate to invest in than just residential. And, since most people are not nearly as comfortable with these other categories, the competition may be a lot less.

Summary of Categories of Real Estate

Residential.

Commercial.

Commercial can be subdivided into:

Office space.

Retail.

Industrial.

Hospitality.

Specialist.

Leasehold.

No land at all.

Mineral rights.

Air space.

ACTION STEPS

1. Drive around your town to look at categories of real estate that until now you have never considered. See if this looking around does anything to your perception of what may be possible.

2. Make a list of the types of real estate that you want to invest in right now. If you want to stick with residential, that is fine; just let yourself know by writing it down. Often by writing something down, we give the statement the force of intent that it did not previously have.

3. Make a list of the types of real estate in which you would like to invest in the future, and put in some target dates. For each type, write down why this category appeals to you.

Chapter 7

FINDING HIDDEN MONEY

DO YOU NEED MONEY TO BUY REAL ESTATE?

Let's get this over with. Yes, you will need money to buy real estate. The question is whether it needs to be your money. That's where financing comes into play. In general, though, you'll need to either provide money for a down payment, have time to design a creative real estate financing deal, or have excellent credit scores that will make a lender feel secure.

If you don't have great credit and you don't have time to develop a creative real estate investment, then you will need to find money. But, it might be easier than you think!

NO MONEY DOWN

"No money down" doesn't mean there's no money down. It means there is none of *your* money in the deal. I've often heard from people who have come across the term "no money down" and assume that means they can go into their local bank and suddenly have 100 percent financing for any deal they bring in. Unfortunately, they get disappointed. It generally doesn't work that way. If you want a no-money-down deal, you will need to go to more creative funding sources. There are three general levels of lender representatives:

1. *Loan officer.* A loan officer works for a bank and has a limited number of loan programs available. If you fit their criteria, you can get a loan. But, if you are self-employed, have credit challenges, or are otherwise a little outside of the norm, you will have difficulty.
2. *Mortgage broker.* We always recommend a mortgage broker or mortgage banker if you need creative financing alternatives. A mortgage broker will have access to hundreds of possible loan programs and so can "shop" programs to find one that fits.
3. *Mortgage banker.* A mortgage banker is the highest level of flexible financing. A mortgage banker has a special license that will allow her to actually put funds together to create packages. These can be the so-called "hard money" loans that call for higher-than-average interest rates. These can also be special programs for large development projects.

CREATIVE FINANCING GETS BUYER A PROPERTY AND A CHECK

One type of loan that a mortgage broker or banker might offer you will actually put money in your pocket at the closing. Here's a real-life story of how it worked for one of Diane's clients at DKA.

Steven's real estate agent showed him a house that was very outdated. The house was on the market for about $250,000 and would require $50,000 worth of work to get it to the average neighborhood value of about $500,000. It was a great deal, but the best deal that Steven could find for financing was 10 percent down on the property. That meant he would have to come up with $75,000 (the 10% down plus the fix-up costs) in cash to do the remodel. Plus, of course, he would have holding costs during the time that he remodeled the property. And, then, he wasn't assured that he would be able to sell it right away and so he wanted to factor in some sales time. All told he estimated that it would take a minimum of 6 months to remodel and then sell the property. He felt that he needed to have a minimum of $90,000 available to do the project. He had about $10,000. What were Steven's options? Steven sat down and listed the possible ways he could come up with the money to do the deal:

- Have the seller participate in the deal.
- Find a "money partner" to participate in the project and give up some of the equity in exchange.
- Find a hard money lender to provide financing at higher terms.
- Find another loan possibility.
- Sell something he owned for the money.
- Put the financing on credit cards.

Before he even finished his list (Dolf and Diane see half a dozen more possibilities for Steven in this example), he realized that he hadn't really searched out loan possibilities yet. Steven met with a new mortgage broker and learned about a type of appraisal called a "value appraisal." His new mortgage broker ordered an appraisal that was based on comparables in the neighborhood as well as a comparison of the costs to complete and the value at the end of the project. The mortgage broker then gave him a conservative 75 percent loan-to-value ratio loan, based on the completed project. That mean that Steven received a loan of $375,000. The lender required that a third party hold back the construction costs, plus a contingency for the holding period and unforeseen circumstances. These were released as money was expensed on the project. When it was all said and done, Steven walked away with a check for $25,000. He also had $100,000 in an escrow account to be used to fix up the project and cover the holding costs. And, of course, he had a property!

If the deal is good enough, you can always find the money.

HARD MONEY ISN'T ALWAYS THE ANSWER

In the success story above, there was something I purposely left out—the terms of the loan. You see in this deal, Steven didn't even care what the interest rate was. He was going to be in and out of the deal so fast (6 months) that the interest was simply a line item expense. Interest is important if you have a very tight deal or if you are planning to hold property for a long period without refinancing.

We recently saw a client walk away from what they had originally thought was the Deal of the Decade. The multifamily apartment building was in a highly appreciating area but it was a burned-out wreck. At first, they had thought that they could do the renovations and then rent it out. But, they found that the rental market was soft. There were too few renters and too many landlords, so most people had to offer special deals to get tenants. Even though the market was appreciating, this particular part of town wasn't. As a result of these negative indicators, the only loan they were able to get was 60 percent loan to value. That meant they needed to come up with 40 percent of the purchase price as a down payment. They didn't have that much money and so went shopping for a hard money lender. They received an offer of 12 percent interest rate for the remainder of the down payment, if they would use additional property as security. By the time they penciled in all of the extra costs, they realized that this wasn't their Deal of the Decade.

SELLER WANTS CASH

So your seller says he wants all cash? It doesn't mean that it needs to be *your* cash. All that means is that the seller has a compelling reason to believe that he needs to be completely paid off and doesn't want to carry back a note.

In some cases, the seller is willing to still carry back a note if it is presented in a way that makes him feel secure. And, in other cases, it's financing or giving up part of the equity to a partner that will give him the cash he needs.

HOW MUCH CASH DO YOU REALLY NEED?

In the simple examples we've used in this book, we generally have counted the down payment based only on the amount left over after the financing. In other words, if you are buying a building for $1,000,000 and you have a loan for 80 percent, you will need to come up with 20 percent—or $200,000—for the down payment. But, that's not the end of the cash requirements. Some of the items that you also need to consider when calculating your cash needs for a property include:

Closing costs.

Fix-up costs.

Holding costs (mortgage payments and utility costs).

Cash reserves.

WHERE TO FIND MONEY

Now, finally, we're to the subject of money. After you've explored all possible financing alternatives and looked for money partners, where can you find money? What assets do you have now that have appreciated? One of the benefits of real estate is that you can take the money out without having to sell the asset. If you've held the property for one or two years (depending on the loan program), you can refinance using a "cash-out" refinance to take excess equity out through a new loan. That's one of the secrets of the leverage of money. Keep your money working, instead of having it tied up in the property.

133

Do you have a pension with money in it? If your plan is under ERISA guidelines, you will not be able to use the money to invest in real estate. ERISA plans include 401(k) plans. But, if your retirement funds are in plans such as SEP-IRAs, you can move the money into a self-directed plan. And, you can then direct that self-directed plan to buy real estate. Not everyone knows about this possible source of funding. Be prepared to shop around a little to find a pension company that will help you set up your self-directed plan to handle real estate. Go to www.DolfAndDiane.com for a list of resources that can help you get your money.

Another source of money might be the underperforming assets you own. These include money market funds, investments in stocks, and even investments in properties. Although generally we recommend that you keep properties to pick up the appreciation, in some cases, it makes more sense to sell.

SELL IT!

Recently Dolf and Diane both recommended that a client sell their property, even though it had a little bit of positive cash flow. The client had bought a single-family residence in northwestern Washington back in 1976 for $45,000. Now, almost 30 years later, it was worth $110,000. Sometimes it makes sense to buy in an area with low appreciation because the rents are high relative to the price. That means that properties will have a good positive cash flow. Not in this case! The property barely provided positive cash flow. Our client asked what we recommended. We both said, in one voice, "Sell it!" Our client now has almost $100,000 in cash to invest in property that will appreciate and provide good cash flow.

SEND MONEY, MOM!

And, if all else fails, you might find a relative with money that he or she wants to invest with you. If it's a loan, treat it like you would a loan from a third party with proper documentation and clear expectations for payment. Otherwise, you might end up on daytime court TV, fighting over the misunderstandings.

Don't let the lack of readily available cash stop you from accumulating your wealth. If the deal is good enough, the money is always available. In fact, if you have trouble with a no-money-down deal, the problem is almost always with the *deal*, not the no-money part.

Possible Sources of Money

Equity in your home.

Equity in other properties.

Pension funds.

Relatives.

Underperforming assets.

The deal itself.

ACTION STEPS

We are going to engage your creativity in the following exercise.

1. List three reasons why you want to make more money in real estate. Get down to the real core reason of why you picked up this book. Some examples of great reasons would be "to create a secure retirement, to build wealth for my family, to contribute more to my favorite charities and causes" and the like. Why are you reading this book? What is it you really want?

   1. _____
   2. _____
   3. _____

2. List 10 reasons why you can't make money in real estate. What is stopping you right now? Some examples might be: I don't have time. My credit is bad. It's impossible to find a deal in my home town. (Most people can come up with four or five options and get so discouraged they stop. Or maybe they can think of only five or six items. Well, this is the book for overachievers. We want you to keep going until you get 10 reasons. By the end of it, you might get really tired of finding reasons why you can't do a no-money-down deal.)

   1. _____
   2. _____
   3. _____
   4. _____
   5. _____
   6. _____

7. _____
8. _____
9. _____
10. _____

3. Now, go back to the list you created above and engage your most creative mind. How can you solve each of these objections? Look for solutions. As a hint, you might find that the last chapter in this book contains some common excuses. For each objection above, list a solution.

4. List five sources of cash you have available to you today (Aunt Tillie, the mattress, someone you know, pension fund).

1. _____
2. _____
3. _____
4. _____
5. _____

5. What one action step can you take this week, based on the information you just reviewed and the questions you just answered?

_____

I commit to performing the above action steps by _____ (date).

Signature:_____

Today's Date: _____

Chapter 8

CREATIVE SOURCES OF FUNDING

At the end of the day, your ability to accumulate a large and lucrative real estate portfolio will be dependent not so much on your ability to find great deals, but rather on your ability to continually find finance for the good deals that you do come across. Since this is such an important component of your real estate strategy, we will explore some more sources of finance and the mindset you need to tap into them in a bit more detail.

As we saw in the previous chapter, seller finance should not be overlooked. If you can get an 80 percent mortgage from the bank, and the seller is willing to leave in 20 percent, then you will have effectively acquired the property with no cash.

So how do you find out if the seller is willing to leave in 20 percent of the purchase price? Let us assure you of one thing. If you don't bring it up, then the chances are very slim that the seller would volunteer, "By the way, how would you like me to leave in 20 percent of my asking price?"

As with many things in life, you have to ask. You have to be bold and say: "Would you consider leaving some money in?," or "Would you consider carrying back a note?" Nine out of ten sellers that you ask may say no, and some may be taken aback or even annoyed. However, every now and then a seller will say "Sure." Maybe they have had trouble selling a property, and have had few or no offers, and your offer (albeit with a note) is still better than nothing. Maybe they do not know what to do with the proceeds of the sale, and they figure that the interest rate you are offering them is more than they would get in the bank.

Dolf was buying a property from a retired couple who were selling the six-bedroom house in which they raised their five children. They wanted to downsize to an apartment with no gardens to maintain or stairs to climb. The asking price on the house was $800,000, and he found out that the apartment they were moving into cost around $400,000. Knowing that they therefore had a lot of spare equity, he asked them if they would consider leaving in a massive $200,000. They looked at each other and said they wanted to discuss it among themselves overnight, and suggested another meeting in the morning. Dolf felt that the possibility of a carryback was slipping away, a view that was reinforced when they got together the next morning and the couple seemed uncomfortable. And then they dropped their bombshell: Would Dolf consider having them leave in $300,000?

You see, with $400,000 cash coming out (the difference between the sale price of their house and the purchase price of their apartment) they knew that the 6 percent interest Dolf was offering them was a lot more than the 2 percent (if that) that they could get in the bank at the time. Never underestimate what motivates your sellers.

Often pride comes into play. Dolf was also involved with the purchase of a large shopping mall in Melbourne. The seller, the elderly head of a dynasty, was adamant that he wanted $124 million for the complex, and wouldn't budge one cent below that, and yet it was appraised at much less. One option was simply to walk away from the deal. But some rudimentary enquiries revealed that the owner had boasted he could get $124 million, and he didn't want to lose face. Eventually a deal was struck with a significant portion of the purchase price being put on deposit with Deutsche Bank at a fixed interest rate for four years. Its value on maturity, when added to the cash portion of the purchase price, enabled the seller to maintain that he got his asking price (he had to ignore the time value of money, of course!). It pays to find out what motivates your sellers.

If a bank is offering you 80 percent finance, and a seller leaves in 20 percent, then you have achieved 100 percent financing. However, what if the bank is offering 80 percent finance, and the seller agrees to leave in 30 percent. Will you not be taking money out of the deal in this case? Of course! And just to counter the nay-sayers, this is perfectly legal.

Now we know that some skeptics will say that banks would never allow that to happen—if they knew you were getting a 30 percent carryback, then they would never agree to an 80 percent loan. However, this is not always the case. There are banks that offer 100 percent financing. There are banks offering 110 percent. We kid you not. The maximum you can borrow at this writing is 125 percent of the purchase price. Now of course there is an expectation that you will spend the surplus on renovations, which in turn will increase the value of the property to give the bank its desired collateral. Just accept that these things do happen, and start letting them happen to you.

Another advantage of real estate over other investments, is that whereas with most other investments you have to pay for any purchases with cash, with real estate you can put anything you like in the contract, and so long as it is accepted by the seller, you have yourself a deal. So, you may not have the cash portion required to purchase a particular property, but there is nothing to stop you offering another property as a down payment. Of course it is your equity in that property that is important, rather than its market value, but sacrificing a smaller property to enable you to acquire a large one may be a good trade-off.

In fact, there is nothing that says you can only barter with other real estate. Dolf and Diane have been party to contracts that have seen all manner of commodities including cars and cruises thrown into the mix. William Zeckendorf, the great real estate tycoon who among other things kept the United Nations in New York by assembling the land for their new headquarters (they were going to shift to Philadelphia in 1946), was contracted to write his biography as part of a lease renewal that he was desperate to transact with a publisher to enable him to buy the building the publishers occupied (they signed the lease, he bought the building, and then he gave them his autobiography).

One technique that can come in handy, especially if no banks will give you a development loan based on a value appraisal as discussed in the previous chapter, is to put in the purchase contract that you agree to close sometime in the future, say in four months' time, and that in the meantime you have the right of access to the property specifically to make improvements. You then go in and "massively increase the value without spending much money," so that by the time you have to close, you can get a new appraisal based on all the work you have done, and hopefully get say an 80 percent loan, which may well be more than the original purchase price.

Of course, you would risk that if you can't make sufficient changes to increase the value to the point that the property becomes self-funding, you will still be committed to buying this property. This is overcome by putting a clause in the contract to buy the property—which we believe you should put in every contract to buy real estate anyway—that this contract is subject to and conditional upon the buyer obtaining finance suitable to the buyer. With this finance clause in place, the only risk now is that you spend money to improve the seller's property and you don't proceed with the acquisition. We believe that this risk is outweighed by the creditability you gain with the seller because you are willing to improve the property before you even take possession. This by itself can help make the deal work.

If a deal is really good, exhaust all possible sources of finance before giving up on it. This may entail approaching family members (don't beg them to give you money; offer them to become your partner). It may involve running an advertisement in the paper, seeking an equity partner or investment partner. It may involve inviting the seller to join you (you put up the land, I will develop it, and from the proceeds you will get the land value, I will get my development costs, and anything that is left over we will split fifty-fifty). It may involve mortgaging your home, other real estate, or other assets that you own. Any debt is risky in that ultimately you have to pay it back. The person who has no debt can never get into the most common financial problem—not paying one's debts. However, having no debt also puts all of one's assets at risk in that if someone were to file a lawsuit against you, be it legitimate, frivolous, or spurious, then all of your assets will be at risk. In this sense, debt actually protects the property owner, because the more debt you have, the less advantageous it would be for someone to file a lawsuit against you. As a bonus, you also have a lot more real estate that is hopefully appreciating in value.

As with all things to do with real estate, you are limited only by your imagination. In fact, the most valuable piece of real estate you have is the six inches, give or take an inch or two, between your right ear and your left ear. What you create in that space determines how successful you will be in the real estate game.

Chapter 9

UNDERSTANDING THE NUMBERS

You've just been handed detailed information on a property. Now quickly decide: Is this the deal of the decade that you must lock up right now, or is this property a real dog that is going to consume time, energy, and money without generating enough income to make it all worthwhile? What information do you need to make the decision?

Once you've mastered the secret of reading the numbers, you will know in a flash whether it's a deal . . . or a dog.

To begin, determine what constitutes a really good deal for you. A good deal might mean you're going to receive a large positive cash flow every month, the property has huge potential for appreciation, or the property offers substantial tax benefits such as abnormally large depreciation write-offs. Alternatively, it could mean that the property has a twist that may greatly improve its value, such as an impending zoning change, extra land that you can subdivide and sell, or a use that no one else has thought of, such as turning an old warehouse into loft apartments.

When you've spotted a deal that seems great, it's time to crunch the numbers. Analysis is something that is best done in the cold light of day without emotional attachment. Investing in real estate is all about the numbers.

UNDERSTANDING THE NUMBERS

What is a property worth? That's not an easy question to answer. In the stock market, value is much easier to ascertain because there is a large market setting value every second for each stock. But, real estate is much more subjective. The profit is often made in the buy. So, it's important to determine the value of a property before you buy and yet it's often very difficult to do so.

A professional appraiser generally looks at one or more of the following factors:

- Comparable values of similar properties recently sold.
- Cost to construct.
- Profitability of the property (if commercial).

And then, after you've accumulated all of that information, how do you decide what is the right information?

A new type of appraisal, called a "value appraisal," has come into vogue recently with real insiders. We have a one-page version of that form (Figure 9.1). You can also go to www.DolfAndDiane.com for a free download of the form.

Property Address: _____
City, State: _____

Asking Price: _____

Comps in Neighborhood: (1) _____ (2)_____
                         (3) _____

CURRENT:

		Instructions to Conducting Your Value Appraisal
Scheduled Rent	_____	1. Complete the amounts under "Current."
Less: Vacancy	_____	
Net Rental Income:	_____	2. Find the capitalization rate (cap rate):
Plus: Other Income	_____	
Total Income	_____	$\text{Cap Rate} = \dfrac{\text{Net Operating Income}}{\text{Purchase Price}}$
Insurance	_____	
Real Estate Taxes	_____	3. Find your cash on cash return (COCR):
Repairs & Maintenance	_____	
Utilities	_____	$\text{COCR} = \dfrac{\text{Yearly Rental Income}}{\text{Down Payment \& Other Expenses}}$
Total Expenses	_____	
		Based on the asking price:
Net Operating Income	_____	
(NOI)		1. Your cap rate is: $ _____
Debt Service (DS)	_____	2. Your COCR is: $ _____
(Principal & Interest)		
Cash Flow	_____	

PROJECTED:

Current value based on comps: _____

Average five-year national appreciation percentage: _____
Average five-year local appreciation percentage: _____

Projected five-year value: _____ to _____

ACTIVE APPRECIATION:

Projected costs to improve: _____ Value after completion: _____

Estimated Value: _____ **to** _____

FIGURE 9.1 The insider's value appraisal form.

On the form, you will see a number of items that you will need to complete. Let's walk through those items together.

Property address. For later reference; fill in the address, city, and state for the property.

Asking price. What is the current asking price?

Comps in neighborhood. The term "comp" refers to comparable values. List the value for three comparable properties that have recently sold. Your real estate agent or appraiser can help you with that information. A common way to review the comparable values is to look at the square footage of the building compared to other buildings. The theory is that if a building is worth $1,000,000 and is 10,000 square feet, then a building that is 20,000 square feet should be worth $2,000,000. Nice theory, but all square footage is not created equal. For example, Diane looked at a house in downtown Phoenix. The neighborhood had a value of $150 per square foot and the house had a 1,000-square-foot basement that was unfinished. If the basement were finished, the house would have an additional 1,000 square feet. But, the basement square footage wasn't as valuable, so it would add only $50,000 to the value. Of course, in this case, it was still a great deal because it would cost less than $20,000 to finish the basement.

Now, go to the column that starts with the heading of *current*.

Scheduled rent. Based on the current rent roll, which is a listing of the units and their rent, list the total annual rental income.

Vacancy. Even in the very best rental area, there will always be vacancies due to someone moving out and the time needed to clean and repair the unit prior to rental.

Net rental income. The net rental income is calculated by subtracting the vacancy amount from the scheduled rent.

Other income. Other income includes other sources of income that might occur for the property. This would include coin-op laundry, storage unit rental, and off-site RV parking.

Total income. Add net rental income and other income to determine total income.

Insurance. Include the estimated insurance cost for the property. You may want to verify the amount of insurance with your own insurance agent. This is a rapidly increasing cost for many real estate investors.

Real estate taxes. Enter the amount of real estate taxes for the property. You can check this out with the assessor's office.

Repairs and maintenance. Sellers will sometimes report lower repair costs. They may also have deferred maintenance, not doing the necessary repairs as they looked forward to selling the property. For now, use your best estimate of repair costs. But, we recommend that you have a professional property inspector help you come up with an accurate number before you close on the property.

Utilities. If the property provides utilities to the tenants or if there is common area, you'll have utility expenses.

Total expenses. Add insurance, real estate taxes, repairs and maintenance, and utilities.

Net operating income (NOI). Net operating income equals total income minus total expenses. This is not the cash flow from the property. This is the income prior to the payment for the property.

Debt service (DS). The principal and interest portion of the payment is considered debt service. If there will be an additional amount withheld for insurance and taxes, do not include that amount here. You've already deducted those items.

Cash flow. Subtract the debt service from NOI to come to cash flow.

Capitalization rate (cap rate). The cap rate reflects the relationship between the NOI and the price of the property. This is a useful way to compare income properties. Calculate the current cap rate based on the asking price and then check out what a normal cap rate in your area would be. Is the price in line? If not, at what price does it seem reasonable based on other properties?

Cash on cash return (COCR). The COCR shows the relationship of annual cash flow divided by the required cash investment. The more money you put into the property, the lower your COCR will be. The COCR calculation ceases to make sense when you buy a property with zero down.

Now look at the *projected* portion of the valuation form.

Current value. Based on the comps you reviewed, what is a reasonable price for this property?

Average five-year national appreciation. Compute the average percentage of appreciation based on the latest data.

Average five-year local appreciation. Calculate the average percentage of appreciation for your area.

Projected five-year value. Multiply each percentage by the current value. What is the estimated range of value in five years?

Now let's go to *active appreciation*.

If this is a property that you expect to remodel or rehabilitate (rehab), enter the projected costs to improve and the estimated value after completion.

Now review all of the data you have put on the form. Based on that information, what is your estimate of the range of value?

Do this exercise for as many properties as possible. The more you do, the more your skills will improve.

CASH ON CASH RETURN

The cash on cash return should be used only as an initial broadview analysis. Do not make this the only calculation that you make when analyzing a property. The problem with the cash on cash analysis is that it loses effectiveness once a property appreciates or if you are able to buy with no money down. Use the COCR for back-of-the-envelope initial calculations. It's a true sign of a novice when you hear them talking only about COCR. It's important, but as the sole indicator it's not very effective.

Interestingly enough, the cash on cash return is effective for about three properties. But, at that point, you'll start losing track of your returns. The coincidence is that this is also the point at which most real estate investors top out in their investment career. The COCR calculation is a great place to start, but if you have already purchased three properties, it's time to learn new ways to calculate returns.

BUYING RETURNS

The case of Tony illustrates what happens when an investor's skills don't keep up with his investing. Tony was like many investors who had gotten stuck at four properties. But, he didn't want to get stuck there. In fact, Tony made a lot of money through his other ventures and so he was accumulating cash that could be used for real estate. Cash on cash was the only analysis point he knew how to do. In fact, he never really learned how to read a property's financial statement. He finally got sick and tired of accumulating cash in a low-yield money market and decided any real estate investment was better than nothing.

He found a large property, but also discovered that it would not create a positive cash flow with a typical down payment. So, Tony decided to actually pay more cash down on the property—opting for a 35 percent down payment instead of the required 20 percent. The difference meant that his property now created a little cash flow. And, unfortunately, Tony gave up on doing any analysis at all because the cash on cash return was so discouraging.

Another solution for Tony would have been to learn about other methods of valuation and analysis. The good news is that he wouldn't even have had to do all of the calculations by hand. There are great computer programs available to do it for you!

Remember that real estate has four types of benefits: passive appreciation, active appreciation, tax benefits, as well as cash flow. The cash on cash return measures only the impact of cash flow. It's an important statistic, but not the only one.

INTERNAL RATE OF RETURN

According to Prentice-Hall, one of the nation's leading publishers of educational material, internal rate of return (IRR) is defined as "the discount rate at which the net present value of a project equals zero." That definition alone might be why most people avoid the IRR calculation!

What that means to the average person is that if the COCR provides you with a snapshot of how a property will perform at any given time, the IRR will give you a motion picture, and will show you how the property performs over an extended period of time. The IRR is much more interesting than COCR, which doesn't allow for good years, bad years, or developing trends. But an IRR calculation does allow for all of these things by taking into account projected rental and capital growth, how much and when mortgage interest will decrease as the principal loan amount is paid off, the effect of depreciation on each year's calculations, your income level, and current tax rates.

"All of that sounds easy in theory," you say, "But how do I know what these amounts will be?" And yes, it is true that working out the IRR is pretty complex, especially when compared to basic yield or COCR. You will, at the very least, need to know the following:

- Property purchase price.
- Property renovation costs.
- True market value of the property.
- Purchase closing costs.
- Property rental income.
- Vacancy rates in the property's neighborhood.
- Expected capital growth rate.
- Expected inflation of expenses and rents in the property location.
- Mortgage interest rate.
- Mortgage structure (i.e., principal and interest, interest only, etc.).
- Mortgage application fee.

- Property management fees.
- Property taxes.
- Property maintenance and repairs.
- Your income level.
- Current federal and state tax rates for persons and businesses.

This is a place where some good software is going to come in handy and make your life as a real estate investor *much* simpler. You should be able to input the amounts that you know, and your projections as to future events, and then have the computer take care of the rest, giving you a printout or chart that indicates future performance. You can see our software recommendations at www.DolfAndDiane.com.

When you start viewing your property with the motion picture of IRR calculation, something as small as a rental increase or decrease of 1 to 2 percent could have larger consequences in the future. A good software program should be able to handle your "what-ifs" and still provide you with a good view of potential future performance.

Methods of Real Estate Analysis

Cap rate: Capitalization rate. Shows the relationship of the net operating income and purchase price.

COCR: Cash on cash return. Measures the initial investment cash return.

IRR: Internal rate of return. The more sophisticated measurement that factors cash return and appreciation to create a "motion picture" for the property.

CAPITALIZATION RATE (CAP RATE)

In real estate appraisal, capitalization is the process of converting income, in the case of real estate net rental income, to a property value. The capitalization rate (*cap rate* for short) determines how rental income capitalizes to capital value. For example, if market cap rates are 10 percent, and you can purchase a property with $12,000 of net income (after all expenses), then that property would be worth $120,000. This means it will take approximately 10 years to recoup the property value from net rental income assuming the rent stays the same. Market cap rates are determined from recent sales. In general, lower cap rates are better for sellers and higher cap rates are better for buyers. However, make sure the neighborhood is good and the property is in decent condition. A high cap rate is of little use if the property is declining in value.

ACTION STEPS

1. Find five investment properties currently for sale either by perusing the classified ads or with the help of a professional, a real estate agent.
2. Complete an Insider's Value Appraisal Form for each property. If you selected single family residences, complete the income section based on anticipated rent.
3. How long did it take you to complete five forms? Dolf has a rule of 100–30–10–1. That means look at 100 properties, offer on 30, get counteroffers on 10, and buy one. What are three things you could do to speed up the process so you

could analyze 100 deals every year . . . or every quarter . . . or every month?

1. _____

2. _____

3. _____

4. How could you make money on a property that you never see?

5. What is the first action step that you want to take after reviewing this chapter and Action Steps?

_____

I commit to performing the above action steps by _____ (date).

Signature:_____

Today's Date: _____

Chapter 10

VALUE ENGINEERING

Most investments are passive, in the sense that once you have bought them, there is very little you can do to increase their value. Whether you are investing in stocks, bonds, treasury bills, mutual funds, unit trusts, certificates of deposit, municipal bonds, baseball cards, phone cards, antiques, gold, silver, platinum, futures, options or commodities, you put up your money (and you generally have to come up with the entire acquisition price in cash) and then hope and pray that whatever you bought does indeed go up.

In this sense, most investments are a bit of a gamble—a gamble that they will go up. It is much like playing roulette in a casino, where you have to put up your own money to gamble on the wheel. The ball has been spun in motion, and at that point all you can do is hope that it lands on one of your bets. There is nothing you can do to influence the outcome of the game (well, nothing legal, anyway). And there is a chance that the ball will fall on a green zero, in which case you forfeit all bets to the casino (even here the analogy is valid, as you can forfeit your investment in a company when it goes bankrupt, although at least with roulette you can buy insurance against this, whereas no insurance company will provide cover against a company going bankrupt).

When it comes to real estate, however, there is seemingly no limit to what you can do to increase the value of your investment. In fact there are so many options that it seems difficult to know where to start.

One of the simplest things you can do is simply to tidy the property. If the grass is one yard high, there is trash littered around along with a rusting car body in the front yard, and a dead tree has fallen over and blocked the driveway, then no appraiser, no matter how visionary, is going to appraise a property in this condition as highly as he or she would after a weekend of general tidying. You may opt to do the work yourself (using the time you would otherwise have spent going to the gym, but then again if you do it yourself, you won't need to go to the gym!) or get contractors, students, or day-laborers in to do the job for you. Here is the interesting thing: The cost of paying someone else to do this work will be a mere fraction of the increased value that the work will foster.

Often a few hundred dollars spent painting a building will increase its value by thousands of dollars. Again, you could do it yourself, or pay someone else to do it. Similarly, new spouting to replace the rusting, half-fallen-down existing eyesores will have a beneficial effect on the property out of proportion to the cost of implementation.

Maybe some windows are cracked, or the door-handle on the front door is all but falling off, or the driveway has pot holes, or a garden shed out back is in danger of falling over, or a bedroom has no windows, or the kitchen is in dire need of re-modeling, or the carpets are worn through, or there is only one power outlet in the living room, or the roof over the verandah leaks, or there is some dry rot in the floor boards, or the kitchen vent doesn't work. You can either say "yuck!" and move on to the next property, or you can get the benefit of a double advantage. First, these deficiencies generally mean that you can buy the property at a discount that is much larger than the deficiencies alone would dictate. For instance, it may only cost $1,000 to paint a house, but in its unpainted state, you may readily get the house for $5,000 or even $10,000 less than if it were painted. It is not just the cost of the paint job that comes into effect, but also the perceived effort involved in getting the job done. And second, by implementing a combination of improvements, not only does the value of the property go up by much more than the cost of making the improvements, but you can now borrow against this increased equity to easily cover all the money spent. In other words, the improvements do not even cost you any money out of your own pocket (the increased mortgage interest is covered by the increased rentals that you can now command).

Dolf often claimed that there were literally 101 things you could do to increase the value of your real estate. Like just about every claim ever made, this one too was challenged, so he set about documenting them. The resulting book, *How to Massively Increase the Value of Your Real Estate Without*

Spending Much Money, has ideas from the simple (replace a dilapidated mailbox with a new one to improve what is often the very first impression people get of a home) to the more esoteric but equally valid (pour a slab of concrete in the front yard of a rambling estate, paint a white circle on it and the letter *H*, and you now have a helipad that may increase the value of the property by $20,000—not bad for $400 of concrete). Dolf concedes it was actually extremely difficult coming up with 101 ideas for this book. It was difficult to limit the ideas to merely 101—there are, of course many more. Check www.DolfAndDiane.com for details on where to get *How to Massively Increase the Value of Your Real Estate Without Spending Much Money*.

If you are excited by the possibility of using your creativity to massively increase value, then you have the makings of an upbeat real estate investor. On the other hand, if you feel stressed out by the prospect of having to actually think and come up with ideas (even those copied from others) then we encourage you to stay out of real estate, buy stocks, and work on improving your hoping skills.

Actually, even if you didn't want to improve real estate, you would still, in our opinion, generally be better off investing in real estate than all the other items listed at the beginning of this chapter, as you would still be getting the tremendous benefit of all the other advantages of real estate over these other investments such as leverage of money, leverage of time, the fact that you can buy real estate below market value, and the fact that you do not have to sell to access some of your profits.

But the ability to massively increase the value of your real estate without spending much money is, to diehard investors like ourselves, too tempting to just let slip by.

ACTION STEPS

1. Consider your own home. Make a list of items that you could improve right now to increase the value of the house, based on what you have just read. Don't just go through the items mentioned above (no room for the helipad so I'll replace the mailbox), but dream up some of your own.
2. Make a list of any investment properties that you may own, and for each one, mentally go through and compile a list of all the improvements you might make that will increase the value of the property by much more than the cost of making the improvements.
3. Next time you visit any investment property you may have, walk through and see if you can add to the list of items that you might improve.
4. Start making the improvements! See if you can have at least one "improvement project" going on at any time. Make it a habit to be continually improving your properties. Habits become addictive. This is a good addiction.
5. The next time you go to look at a piece of real estate with a view to possibly buying it, think about what you may do to increase its value once you have acquired it. Often a deal may be marginal as is, but once you factor in how you may increase its value with relatively little effort, it may suddenly become a viable proposition.

I commit to performing the above action steps by _____ (date).

Signature:_____

Today's Date: _____

Chapter 11

CYCLE OF A PROPERTY

THREE CYCLES OF A PROPERTY

We've gone through many steps involved in finding a property. Now, it's time to put all of the information together into a tangible plan that you can use to make money in real estate! The simple *three-cycle system* for property started from a conversation with Morgan Smith, founder of Morgan Capital. Morgan, at 33 years of age, has 60 offices and over 650 employees and yet still finds time to invest in his own real estate. He doesn't have time to waste on unnecessary steps. That's why this simple system is so effective.

The three cycles of action for a property are:

1. Take it down.
2. Stabilize it.
3. Put it on the shelf.

TAKE IT DOWN

"Take it down" quite simply means *buy it*. Remember, that is the ultimate goal of all of these exercises—to find real estate that will provide you the benefit you want and then buy it.

There are actually six steps to the take-it-down cycle:

1. *Find it.* Clearly establish what you are looking for and then enlist the help of professionals (real estate agents) to help you find properties. You can spend your time looking as well, but you'll find that you spend an inordinate amount of time in this one step. Plus, if you're the one who found the deal, there is the risk that you will then do the analysis with a slant toward trying to make the deal work. If someone else brings you the deal, it is easier to stay objective.

2. *Evaluate it.* Use the information found earlier in the book to complete the Insider's Value Appraisal Form.

3. *Lock it up.* If the property passes your tests so far, lock it up with a refundable earnest money deposit. Make sure that your contract gives you plenty of ways out of the deal if the property doesn't meet your specifications as you investigate further. Don't put a nonrefundable deposit down until the property has passed the due diligence phase. In the vernacular of seasoned real estate investors, don't go "hard" on the money until the deal is certain. Common contingencies are: financing, physical inspection, and clear title. Until you've signed off on these items, you can still get out of the deal.

4. *Due diligence.* The property is now locked up and you have a specified number of days according to the contract

in order to do your due diligence. The better your due diligence, the more certain you will feel about the final decision you make on the property. A sample due diligence form is available in Figure 11.1.

5. *Final decision.* Now is the time to decide. Do you want the property or not? Now is also a good time to check in with your lenders and closing agents to verify that your closing date is still good and to verify that the lender is happy with the property after you've done your due diligence. If you find that the closing date might be unrealistic, communicate that immediately to your real estate agent or seller. If a loan gets held up, it's not the end of the world. If it's still a deal you want, you might need to add additional funds to the earnest money to keep the seller happy. We've also sometimes had to go "hard" on part of the money so that a portion of the earnest money becomes nonrefundable. That can be a scary time, but if you've got good team members, good communication, and have properly done the analysis, you'll be fine! Interestingly enough, the bigger the property, the easier the close. But the due diligence phase can go on for months.

6. *Buy it.* The final action of the first cycle seems almost anticlimactic. Or, at least, if you've done your homework, it will be calm. You will hopefully use a closing agent who will prepare the documents, calculate the prorations, and escrow the money.

STABILIZE IT

Occasionally, you'll buy a property that is a cash cow from the first day. You don't need to do anything to make it work better.

1. RESIDENTIAL PROPERTY DISCLOSURE CHECKLIST

Don't let anyone tell you that investing doesn't require some hard work on your part! Carrying out a detailed due diligence report will take time, but when you're finished you will be in the position to make an informed decision about potential properties. We have broken our *due diligence checklists* out into two categories—buying residential properties and buying commercial properties. We've also added a third checklist, which deals specifically with environmental issues. As you gather the information, check it off your list.

What is your objective for this property?

Ask Yourself . . .	Answers and Notes
☐ Long-term hold?	_____
☐ Rehabilitation project?	_____
☐ Quick flip?	_____
☐ Personal residence?	_____
☐ Development?	_____
☐ Other?	_____

Seller Information

Questions to Ask and Information to Get	Answers and Notes
☐ The name, address, phone number, and business number of the seller.	_____
☐ How long has the property been on the market?	_____
☐ If the property was previously listed, for how long was it on the market before?	_____
☐ Why is the owner selling the property?	_____

Property Exterior and Lot Condition

Questions to Ask and Information to Get	Answers and Notes
☐ Property purchase price.	_____
☐ Street address of the property.	_____
☐ Square footage of the lot.	_____
☐ Size of yard(s).	_____
☐ Legal description of the property.	_____

FIGURE 11.1 Real estate due diligence checklists.

Property Exterior and Lot Condition

Questions to Ask and Information to Get	Answers and Notes
☐ Extent and condition of landscaping.	_____
☐ Is there an in-ground sprinkler system, and what condition is it in?	_____
☐ Does the property have an in-ground or above-ground swimming pool, and if so, what condition is it in?	_____
☐ Does property have fencing, and what condition is the fencing in?	_____
☐ Schools, and school proximity.	_____
☐ Shopping opportunities and access.	_____
☐ Zoning of property.	_____
☐ Value of comparable properties in the neighborhood?	_____
☐ Estimated income/size of area families.	_____
☐ Estimated area population growth.	_____

Property Structure(s) and Interior

Questions to Ask and Information to Get	Answers and Notes
☐ Builder (check credentials with the local contractors association and the Better Business Bureau).	_____
☐ Age of structure.	_____
☐ Condition and type of construction inside and outside.	_____
☐ Condition of wiring.	_____
☐ Condition of plumbing.	_____
☐ Condition of foundation.	_____
☐ Insulation up to code/storm windows, doors.	_____
☐ What, if any, repairs are needed?	_____
☐ Have any additions been made, and are all additions properly permitted?	_____
☐ Square footage of structure.	_____
☐ Number of floors and square footage per floor.	_____
☐ How many bedrooms and how many bathrooms does the building have?	_____
☐ What other rooms does the building have? List rooms and describe condition of each.	_____

FIGURE 11.1 *(Continued)*

Property Structure(s) and Interior

Questions to Ask and Information to Get	Answers and Notes
☐ Is there an alarm system? Is it owned or leased, and will it remain after the sale?	_____
☐ What are the kitchen appliances, and what condition are they in? Are they all remaining with the property?	_____
☐ Inventory of what room furniture, fixtures, draperies, window covers, etc. are staying.	_____
☐ Is there a garage? How large is it? How many cars can fit inside? What condition is the garage in?	_____
☐ Does the property have a view, and if so, what kind of a view does it have?	_____
☐ Is there a fireplace, and if so, what is its current condition? When was the chimney last cleaned?	_____
☐ What kind of flooring? If there is carpeting, what condition is it in?	_____
☐ How many windows does the building have and what condition are they in?	_____

Roof

Questions to Ask and Information to Get	Answers and Notes
☐ Condition of roof.	_____
☐ How old is roof.	_____
☐ Any problems with roof/leakage? When?	_____
☐ Roof composition.	_____
☐ Any repair/resurfacing of roof? When?	_____

Heating/Air Conditioning/Electrical

Questions to Ask and Information to Get	Answers and Notes
☐ Date heating system installed.	_____
☐ Condition of heating system.	_____
☐ Type of heating system and make. Is it gas or electric?	_____
☐ Date of last heating system inspection and/or service.	_____

FIGURE 11.1   *(Continued)*

Heating/Air Conditioning/Electrical

Questions to Ask and Information to Get	Answers and Notes
☐ Does the structure have air conditioning? What type of system is it? What is its cooling capacity, and what condition is the A/C system in?	_____
☐ Date of last A/C inspection and/or service.	_____
☐ What type of ventilation system? Is it acceptable?	_____
☐ Condition of electrical equipment.	_____
☐ Available voltage.	_____
☐ Date of last electrical equipment inspection and/or service.	_____
☐ What are the monthly utility, heating, and cooling costs for both winter and summer?	_____
☐ Is the insulation up to code?	_____
☐ Are there any known defects to any of these systems? Describe.	_____

Water/Sewer

Questions to Ask and Information to Get	Answers and Notes
☐ Water supply source? City, septic tank, etc.	_____
☐ Condition of water supply.	_____
☐ Known prior plumbing leaks/rust problems.	_____
☐ Any flooding? When? How was it repaired?	_____
☐ Any drainage problems? Describe.	_____
☐ Condition of landscape sprinklers? Describe.	_____
☐ Type of water pipes (copper, lead, PVC, etc.).	_____
☐ Any water pressure problems?	_____
☐ Known standing-water areas.	_____
☐ Adequate drainage/roof, ground.	_____
☐ Condition and age of water heater.	_____
☐ Last date water heater inspected and/or serviced?	_____
☐ What company did inspection?	_____
☐ Capacity of water heater?	_____
☐ Location of water heater?	_____

FIGURE 11.1 *(Continued)*

Water/Sewer

Questions to Ask and Information to Get	Answers and Notes
☐ Safety device for water heater?	_____

Hazards

Questions to Ask and Information to Get	Answers and Notes
☐ Home insurance.	_____
☐ Are there any pending legal actions or liens?	_____
☐ Are there any restrictions on property use?	_____
☐ Are there any easements on the property?	_____
☐ Is the property in a designated flood or other hazard zone?	_____
☐ Are there any previous inspection reports? If so, get copies.	_____
☐ Are there any previous pest inspection reports? If so, get copies.	_____
☐ Any problems with stability of ground beneath property, settling, cracks in cement, etc.?	_____
☐ Any known present or future problems affecting the property?	_____
☐ Are there any known or future problems on nearby properties?	_____
☐ Is there any pending expansion or real estate development planned for the area?	_____
☐ Is property leased? If so, when does the lease expire?	_____
☐ Does anyone have a right of first refusal or option to buy after the lease expires?	_____

Loan Information

Questions to Ask and Information to Get	Answers and Notes
☐ Lender's name.	_____
☐ Name of person or entity on title as owner.	_____
☐ Is the current loan assumable? If it is, will it require a purchaser to qualify?	_____
☐ Current loan number?	_____
☐ Current loan interest rate.	_____

FIGURE 11.1   *(Continued)*

175

Loan Information

Questions to Ask and Information to Get	Answers and Notes
☐ Original loan amount? When granted?	_____
☐ Balance of original loan.	_____
☐ Closing costs, if you assume loan?	_____
☐ Is there a second? Can it be discounted?	_____
☐ Are there any balloon payments due under mortgage, and if so, how much and when?	_____
☐ Is there any mortgage prepayment penalty?	_____
☐ Will seller help finance or pay points?	_____
☐ If you don't assume, what is new loan amount?	_____
☐ Length of new loan?	_____
☐ Monthly payment amount of new loan?	_____
☐ Insurance costs and requirements for new loan?	_____
☐ Home guarantee?	_____
☐ CC&R's/restrictions.	_____
☐ Move-in date?	_____

Purchase Fees

Questions to Ask and Information to Get	Answers and Notes
☐ How much are application fees?	_____
☐ How much will appraisal fees cost?	_____
☐ How much will loan fees cost?	_____
☐ How much will recording fees be?	_____
☐ Are you required to furnish a credit report, and if so, how much will that cost?	_____
☐ What will escrow fees be?	_____
☐ Points? How much?	_____

FIGURE 11.1 *(Continued)*

**Cash Flow Estimate and Problem Points
(Make sure you verify all of the amounts in
this section.)**

Questions to Ask and Information to Get	Answers and Notes
☐ What is the current rental income for the property?	_____
☐ Has the property sat vacant? If so, how much rental income was lost due to vacancies?	_____
☐ Conduct a rent check by knocking on doors and asking around in neighborhood.	_____
☐ What have the homeowner's insurance costs been historically? Have prior claims impacted insurance costs?	_____
☐ Order a C.L.U.E. report from www.choicetrust.com.	_____
☐ How will property management be handled, by you or by a separate management company? What are those costs?	_____
☐ What is the assessed value of the property?	_____
☐ What is the yearly tax amount? Is that likely to become subject to sudden increases?	_____
☐ Review title report and title insurance.	_____
☐ Arrange for structural and pest inspections to confirm condition of property and establish repairs and maintenance needed so you can estimate yearly and deferred repairs.	_____

FIGURE 11.1 *(Continued)*

2. COMMERCIAL PROPERTY DISCLOSURE CHECKLIST

What is your objective with this property?

Questions to Ask and Information to Get	Answers and Notes
☐ Long-term hold?	_____
☐ Rehabilitation project?	_____
☐ Quick flip?	_____
☐ Development?	_____
☐ Other?	_____

Seller Information

Questions to Ask and Information to Get	Answers and Notes
☐ The name, address, phone number, and business number of the seller.	_____
☐ How long has the property been on the market?	_____
☐ If the property was previously listed, for how long was it on the market before?	_____
☐ Why is the owner selling the property?	_____

Property Exterior and Lot Condition

Questions to Ask and Information to Get	Answers and Notes
☐ Property purchase price.	_____
☐ Street address of the property.	_____
☐ Square footage of the lot.	_____
☐ Is there a storefront, and if so, what is its square footage?	_____
☐ Is there adequate parking? What is the condition of parking lot?	_____
☐ Legal description of the property.	_____
	_____
☐ Map of area showing property plot.	_____
☐ Extent and condition of landscaping?	_____
☐ Zoning and zoning restrictions.	_____
☐ Covenants and usage restrictions.	_____

FIGURE 11.1 *(Continued)*

Property Exterior and Lot Condition

Questions to Ask and Information to Get	Answers and Notes
☐ Value of comparable properties in the neighborhood?	_____
☐ Loading docks/access?	_____
☐ Easy access to building? Is it up to ADA standard?	_____
☐ Closeness to main roads/freeway/bus line.	_____
☐ Foot traffic in front of building.	_____
☐ Population within range of business.	_____
☐ Condition of streets/neighborhood.	_____
☐ Area traffic patterns.	_____

Lease Information

Questions to Ask and Information to Get	Answers and Notes
☐ Landlord's name.	_____
☐ How much is the rent? How many and when are installments due?	_____
☐ How much time is left on the original lease? Can it be renewed? Will there be a rent increase, and if so, how much?	_____
☐ Option to buy/renew/first refusal?	_____
☐ Are there any tax payment clauses in the lease?	_____
☐ Type of lease? Original or sublease.	_____
☐ Is the rent based on square footage in the building only or is any frontage included?	_____
☐ Who performs maintenance/interior, exterior, landscaping, and who pays for it?	_____
☐ Get copies of lease agreements.	_____

Service Costs under Lease

Questions to Ask and Information to Get	Answers and Notes
☐ Services provided by landlord?	_____
☐ Water and garbage service and costs?	_____

FIGURE 11.1 *(Continued)*

Service Costs under Lease

Questions to Ask and Information to Get	Answers and Notes
☐ Security costs?	
☐ Equipment cost/rental cost, depreciation.	_____
☐ Heating/air conditioning?	_____
☐ Electric/gas?	_____

Loan Information

Questions to Ask and Information to Get	Answers and Notes
☐ Lender's name.	_____
☐ Name of person or entity on title as owner.	_____
☐ Is the current loan assumable? If it is, will it require a purchaser to qualify?	_____
☐ Current loan number.	_____
☐ Current loan interest rate.	_____
☐ Original loan amount? When granted?	_____
☐ Balance of original loan.	_____
☐ Closing costs, if you assume loan?	_____
☐ Is there a second? Can it be discounted?	_____
☐ Are there any balloon payments due under mortgage, and if so, how much and when?	_____
☐ Is there any mortgage prepayment penalty?	_____
☐ Will seller help finance or pay points?	_____
☐ If you don't assume, what is new loan amount?	_____
☐ Length of new loan?	_____
☐ Monthly payment amount of new loan?	_____
☐ Insurance costs and requirements for new loan?	_____
☐ Building guarantee?	_____
☐ CC&R's/restrictions.	_____
☐ Move-in date?	_____

FIGURE 11.1   *(Continued)*

Property Structure and Interior

Questions to Ask and Information to Get	Answers and Notes
☐ Builder and architect (check credentials with the local contractors association and the Better Business Bureau).	
☐ Age of structure.	_____
☐ Condition and type of construction inside and outside.	
☐ Condition of wiring.	_____
☐ Condition of plumbing.	_____
☐ Condition of basement foundation.	_____
☐ Insulation up to code?	_____
☐ What, if any, repairs are needed?	_____
☐ Have any additions been made, and are all additions properly permitted?	
☐ Square footage of structure.	_____
☐ Number of floors and square footage per floor.	_____
☐ How many bathrooms does the building have on each floor?	
☐ What other rooms does the building have? List rooms and describe condition of each.	
☐ Is there an alarm system? Is it owned or leased, and will it remain after the sale?	
☐ What kind of flooring? If there is carpeting, what condition is it in?	
☐ How many windows does the building have and what condition are they in?	
☐ What type of internal fire protection/overhead sprinkler system is installed, and what condition is it in? How many sprinkler heads per floor? Is it up to current code standards?	

Heating/Air Conditioning/Electrical

Questions to Ask and Information to Get	Answers and Notes
☐ Date heating system installed.	_____
☐ Condition of heating system.	_____
☐ Type of heating system and make. Is it gas or electric?	

FIGURE 11.1   *(Continued)*

181

Heating/Air Conditioning/Electrical

Questions to Ask and Information to Get	Answers and Notes
☐ Date of last heating system inspection and/or service.	
☐ Does the structure have air conditioning? What type of system is it? What is its cooling capacity, and what condition is the A/C system in?	
☐ Date of last A/C inspection and/or service.	
☐ What type of ventilation system? Is it acceptable?	
☐ Condition of electrical equipment.	
☐ Available voltage.	
☐ Date of last electrical equipment inspection and/or service.	
☐ What are the monthly utility, heating, and cooling costs for both winter and summer?	
☐ Is the insulation up to code?	
☐ Are there any known defects to any of these systems? Describe.	

Water and Sewer

Questions to Ask and Information to Get	Answers and Notes
☐ Water supply source? City, septic tank, etc.	
☐ Condition of water supply.	
☐ Known prior plumbing leaks/rust problems.	
☐ Any flooding? When? How was it repaired?	
☐ Any drainage problems? Describe.	
☐ Condition of landscape sprinklers? Describe.	
☐ Type of water pipes (copper, lead, PVC, etc.)	
☐ Any water pressure problems?	
☐ Known standing-water areas.	
☐ Adequate drainage/roof, ground.	
☐ Condition and age of water heater.	
☐ Last date water heater inspected and/or serviced?	
☐ What company did inspection?	
☐ Capacity of water heater?	

FIGURE 11.1 *(Continued)*

Water and Sewer

Questions to Ask and Information to Get	Answers and Notes
☐ Location of water heater?	_____
☐ Safety device for water heater?	_____

Cash Flow Estimate and Problem Points (Make sure you verify all of the amounts in this section.)

Questions to Ask and Information to Get	Answers and Notes
☐ What is the current rental income for the property?	_____
☐ Has the property or units within the property sat vacant? If so, how much rental income was lost due to vacancies?	_____
☐ Conduct a rent check by reviewing neighborhood commercial rental rates.	_____
☐ What have the building insurance costs been historically? Have prior claims impacted insurance costs?	_____
☐ Order a C.L.U.E. report from www.choicetrust.com.	_____
☐ How will property management be handled, by you or by a separate management company? What are those costs?	_____
☐ What is the assessed value of the property?	_____
☐ What is the yearly tax amount? Is that likely to become subject to sudden increases?	_____
☐ Review title report and title insurance.	_____
☐ Arrange for structural and pest inspections to confirm condition of property and establish repairs and maintenance needed so you can estimate yearly and deferred repairs.	_____

FIGURE 11.1   *(Continued)*

3. ENVIRONMENTAL CONDITIONS DISCLOSURE CHECKLIST

If you are considering the purchase of a commercial property that has been used for things like a gas station, a dry cleaning shop, an auto paint and/or repair facility, a plant nursery, or a manufacturing and storage facility, there are special precautions that you should take. In addition to Forms 1 and 2, make sure you also complete Form 3 if there are any environmental factors that need to be taken into consideration as a part of your decision.

Environmental Information

Questions to Ask and Information to Get	Answers and Notes
☐ Standard Industrial Classification number.	_____
☐ Was recycling done on the property?	_____
☐ Are there any claims against owner for shipping waste?	_____
☐ Are there any prior claims against owner?	_____
☐ Are all necessary permits in place?	_____
☐ When was the last site check?	_____
☐ Was there hazardous waste on the property?	_____
☐ How was it stored and disposed of?	_____
☐ Are there any underground tanks?	_____
☐ Was there any spillage or known leaks?	_____
☐ Was there any known contamination to water or ground on this property?	_____
☐ Water pollution history.	_____

Documents to Review

Information to Get	Questions and Notes
☐ Primary use description.	_____
☐ Regulations/requirements, local, state, federal.	_____
☐ Ownership history/detail.	_____
☐ Complaints by citizens.	_____
☐ Contracts with disposal services, waste transport.	_____
☐ Insurance coverage/claims for environmental loss with resolution.	_____
☐ Pending litigation.	_____
☐ Judgments, settlement agreements.	_____
☐ Operating permits.	_____

FIGURE 11.1 *(Continued)*

Documents to Review

Information to Get	Questions and Notes
☐ Maps, aerial photos, diagrams, technical reports.	
☐ Environmental assessments, Phase I and II reports.	
☐ Reports on produced pollutants.	
☐ Description of noncompliance penalties.	
☐ Environmental violators.	

Reports and Citations (Ask if there are any reports available in these areas, and if there have ever been any citations issued for noncompliance. If there have been, make sure you get copies.)

Questions to Ask and Information to Get	Notes
☐ Geotechnical.	
☐ Water quality.	
☐ Sanitation Department.	
☐ Hazardous Material Site Characterization.	
☐ Air quality.	
☐ Department of Health Services.	
☐ Environmental Protection Agency.	

Setting

Questions to Ask and Information to Get	Answers and Notes
☐ Type of soil.	
☐ Soil stains.	
☐ Destination of surface water runoff.	
☐ Healthy vegetation.	
☐ Groundwater depth.	

FIGURE 11.1 *(Continued)*

Facility Use?
**(If the facilities were used for any of the five categories
listed below, or if any of the goods listed below were
stored on the property, make sure you get a full
description of the types of chemicals that have been
used and storage procedures for all chemicals.)**

Questions to Ask and Information to Get	Answers and Notes
☐ Dry cleaning.	_____
☐ Plant nursery.	_____
☐ Gas station.	_____
☐ Paint/repair of automobile.	_____
☐ Manufacture, storage, etc. of:	_____
• Photocopiers.	_____
• Glue/rubber products.	_____
• Pesticides and/or fertilizer.	_____
• Furniture/wood preservatives.	_____
• Plastics and/or foams.	_____
• Chemicals or explosives.	_____
• Glass.	_____
• Semiconductors and electrical devices.	_____
• Detergents and/or soaps.	_____
• Paper products and/or pulp.	_____
• Jewelry/metal plating or products.	_____
• Petroleum products.	_____
• Paint.	_____
• Auto parts.	_____

FIGURE 11.1 *(Continued)*

But, often there is work to do. That's why you got such a great deal on it in the first place!

Use the value engineering techniques you have learned to get the biggest benefit from the money you invest in your property. Above all, ask yourself with every expenditure, "How will this improve the property?" We've seen new real estate investors get very caught up in the fix-up stage to the point where they've lost all sight of what the outcome really is. Basically, you want a stable "turnkey" property. It generally takes up to six months to stabilize a property. The bigger the property, the longer the time needed to settle it out.

PUT IT ON THE SHELF

You've bought your property and you've stabilized it. Now, enjoy the fruits of your labor and wait. We recommend that you determine critical points for your property so that you can actually step back from worrying about daily analysis of the property. Some of the critical points you might establish are:

- Gross rent collected.
- Vacancy rate.
- Repair costs.
- Utility costs.
- Minimum cash flow.
- Equity buildup.

The goal is to determine when it is time to refinance, when it is time to review the current property management, and when it is time to exit the property.

ACTION STEPS

1. Work through the first four steps of the take-it-down cycle (find it, evaluate it, lock it up, and due diligence) on at least one property in the next month. When you have completed those four steps come back and complete the final two action steps for this month.

2. What were your feelings after going through those six steps? Did you follow through on buying the property? Why or why not?

3. What do you need to do to ensure that you have one profitable real estate property within the next three months?

I commit to performing the above action steps by _____ (date).

Signature:_____

Today's Date: _____

PART THREE

Secrets of Success through Teams

Chapter 12

DESIGNING YOUR TEAM

DO YOU NEED A TEAM?

Take a look at any group of experienced real estate investors. When they're asked how many own at least one real estate property, all hands shoot up. Then as they're progressively asked how many have two, three, four, and five the number of hands drastically falls off. In a room full of experienced real estate investors, less than 10 percent own more than four or five properties.

The difference between handling one or two properties and handling more than five is the ability to leverage time and effort with a productive and efficient team. Unfortunately, if we weren't taught about financial matters in school, we certainly weren't taught to design, interview, and then build an effective team.

To go from one property to 100, you will absolutely need to leverage your time through the use of a team. The question that we hear screaming at us is "How do I find the members of my team?" Well, before we show you how, will you commit to finding and building your own team? In other words, are you merely interested or fully committed? The answer will determine whether you end up owning closer to one property or closer to 100.

Finding the right members for your team can be a frustrating and arduous process. However, when you do have the right team in place it will save you so much time, effort, and worry that it will make the process worthwhile.

EDUCATE YOURSELF FIRST

Assume you want to hire a rocket propulsion scientist. How would you do so? Which attributes would you be looking for? What questions would you ask to make sure a candidate really knew her field? Surely it is safe to conclude that it is much easier to make a decision when you know a lot about rocket propulsion than if you don't even know what a rocket is.

You don't need to be a rocket scientist to understand real estate. But, it pays to understand some basics of real estate before hiring professionals for your team. For instance, if you've just bought your first investment property and you're considering getting a property manager to manage this property—everything from potential tenant screening to maintenance to collecting the rent—then, given you've never owned an investment property before, how will you know which questions to ask a potential property manager? Anything that a prospective manager tells you will probably sound plausible. However, by managing your first property yourself (or maybe your first two, three, or even four), you'll learn all the smart things to do and the painful mistakes to avoid. For example, you might get burned by a bad tenant. You'll learn the importance of background and credit checks. As a result of managing your own properties for a period of time, you'll know the questions to ask when you interview a prospective property manager.

Similarly, we think it pays to have an attempt at doing your own bookkeeping, maintenance, and rehabbing. A few people have a flair for these activities and can do them efficiently and with enjoyment. However, for most of us, we soon realize that one or more of these activities are not our passion or primary talent and that it would be smarter to pay other people to do these things. The whole point is that by having some experience (no matter how trying the process might have been) you are far better equipped to choose good team members.

In general, some experience will help you select a good team member. However, when it comes to selling a property, while you can do it yourself, to us it makes more sense to use a real estate agent. A real estate agent will have a huge database of potential buyers, facilities to list the properties on national registrars of properties for sale, and systems in place to facilitate closing the deal and transacting the property through to completion. Most importantly, the selling of real estate can be very time consuming, and instead of showing your property to multitudes of tire kickers before finding a buyer, all to save a commission, you could have been out there doing four other deals!

LEARN TO BE A GOOD INTERVIEWER

We've shown you the importance of learning about a subject before employing people. When interviewing potential managers, bookkeepers, and the like, you still need to ask them how they do things. The difference is that you are no longer asking these questions to discover the answer, but to find out what they know. Because you have some experience, you're better able to assess their abilities.

It's also good to give direction to your team members. Don't assume that they know what you want. For example, if you ask them, "What is a good investment?" you have not given them enough information to adequately answer the question. Does "good" mean strong cash flow or strong appreciation? Are you looking for a large commercial building or a single-family residence? Are you looking to create long-term passive income or cash from a quick flip? A good deal for one person is not necessarily a good deal for another.

The Insider's Speed Method for Building a Great Team

- A well-lead team can do more than one person can.
- Know the subject.
- Ask good questions.
- Two good specialists are better than one.
- A little competition can be a good thing.
- Show appreciation for a job well done.

WHO SHOULD BE ON YOUR TEAM?

The specialists you need on your team will vary, but here are the people we wouldn't invest without:

- *Real estate agent.* The real estate agent is listed first because they are often the ones who start the whole thing going! You can use a real estate agent to locate property to buy, prove market comparable values, estimate margin for active appreciation, pull statistics for past appreciation, and sell properties.
- *Property manager.* A property manager is a critical team member for large multifamily units and commercial properties. Many people also use property managers for single-family residential rentals. Not all property managers are created equal, nor are the services they provide the same. For example, Diane hired a property manager to find her a tenant for one of her out-of-state single-family homes. She paid a flat fee for that service once a tenant was located, screened, and placed in the home. However, the property manager did not continue with any services. Diane had a good handyman in the area who could handle repairs at a lesser cost. Don't be afraid to ask for what you want from the property manager!
- *Closing agent.* The title company or real estate attorney is an integral part of your real estate wealth-building team. They will search the title for the property to make sure there are no hidden encroachments on the property or title. They will also provide title insurance that guarantees the property has transferred properly. Do not underestimate the value of the title insurance!

- *Mortgage broker.* The lender is an integral part of our teams. They can help you create your overall investment plan. A good mortgage broker who also invests can make you a fortune! One day, Diane's mortgage broker called her with a property he said she just had to buy. She bought it on his recommendation and in seven years the property has tripled in value.

- *CPA/tax specialist.* The tax benefits from real estate are huge . . . if your advisors know what they are doing. Your responsibility is to select knowledgeable advisors, provide current and accurate information to them, and to keep them posted on possible new purchases. Then, pay attention to the advice they give you! If you have real estate and either you or your spouse can qualify as a real estate professional and you still pay tax, there is one of two problems: (1) You don't own enough real estate, or (2) you aren't taking advantage of all of the tax benefits of real estate. Not all CPAs understand real estate. If you're serious about investing in real estate, make sure your CPAs understand what you're doing.

- *Attorney.* We think it's a good idea to keep a good relationship with a top attorney. You don't want to be searching for an attorney when you just suddenly found that you have a problem with a transaction, a tenant, or even a contract. Maintain a good relationship with an attorney who understands real estate and hopefully even personally invests.

- *Insurance.* In some states today, the biggest barrier to buying property is finding property insurance! In some areas, it is now almost impossible to find insurance for properties that have had water damage, for example. Make a good property insurance agent part of your team so that you can call her whenever you need some help.

- *Contractors (if not through your property managers).* If your property manager doesn't furnish a handyman, make sure you have someone. You'll also want to have the name of a couple of contractors that you trust and that you can call when you need them for rehab work or repairs.

MISTAKES IN TRANSFERRING TITLE

Besides all the problems you can encounter by buying a negative cash-flowing property or a property with hidden structural problems, the biggest risk of all might occur with how you take title. Imagine buying a property and then finding out you really haven't bought it in the way you thought you had. Here are some common mistakes:

- *Mistake #1:* Quitclaiming property without considering tax ramifications. A quitclaim is an easy-to-complete document that you can pick up at an office supply house. Anyone can quitclaim a property. But, changing the title on a property from one person to another using this method can trigger a gift tax of over 50 percent!
- *Mistake #2:* Not realizing that using a quitclaim deed also voids the title insurance.
- *Mistake #3:* Not using title insurance on a purchase.

Imagine finding out later that the property you thought was yours really has easements running through it or has liens recorded that you must pay! If you have title insurance and you didn't know about those things, the insurance will pay. If you don't have title insurance, the problems are all yours. Avoid these problems by always using qualified professionals to handle your property transactions.

A colleague recently told us the story of a woman who had decided to save $1,000 on using a closing agent and instead handled the property transaction herself. She had paid $200,000 for a property 10 years ago. Now she was selling the house and she was going through a title company to do so. She said that the house was free and clear and that she had owned the house for 10 years. Imagine everyone's surprise when they discovered that she had not properly drawn up the deed 10 years ago. She didn't even own the house. Luckily, she was able to find the prior owner and got him to sign the proper documents. Can you imagine what would have happened if he had died and she now had to deal with an estate? Or what if he was in bankruptcy? Or what if he had recently gone through a divorce? The "what-ifs" in this case are almost staggering. She was very lucky in the result she got. And, it's a lesson we can all learn from. Use the professionals and always buy title insurance so that your risk has been minimized.

ACTION STEPS

1. List the members of your current team.

_____

_____

_____

2. Who else do you need to add to your team?

_____

_____

(Continued)

(Continued)

3. What qualifications would these people need?

_____

_____

_____

4. What is one action step you can take right now to create a better team?

_____

I commit to performing the above action steps by _____ (date).

Signature:_____

Today's Date: _____

Chapter 13

INTERVIEWING TEAM MEMBERS

Once you've identified the people you need on your team, how do you go about finding them? Without a doubt, questions related to finding good real estate agents, property managers, accountants, and attorneys are the single biggest group of questions that we get. The fact is, it's hard to find good people. And, it's even harder to find them if you don't know where to look or what to ask them once you think you've found them.

HOW TO FIND TEAM MEMBERS

A simple web site search on any of these types of advisors will bring up thousands of references for you. However, here are several that we feel are great places for you to begin searching for your local team of advisors.

Property Managers

The National Association of Residential Property Managers (http://narpm.net) and the Institute of Real Estate Management (www.irem.org) provide an extensive network for professional property managers as well as resources for property owners seeking managers, matching service, and the like.

Real Estate Agents

The National Association of Realtors (www.realtor.org) lists an extensive network of nationwide Realtors, along with resources for buyers, sellers, and investors.

Real Estate Investment Clubs

A real estate investment club can be a tremendous resource to meet other investors and advisors in your area. In fact, you can sometimes hear about great real estate deals from your fellow members. Diane made $70,000 on a property she heard about from a real estate investment club. Here are some Web resources for real estate investment clubs:

www.real-estate-online.com.

www.reiclub.com.

www.realestatelink.net.

Birds of a Feather

The old saying is that birds of a feather flock together. The same is true of good advisors. Good accountants will know good attorneys (and bad attorneys). If you've found someone you can work with because they have a level of expertise you appreciate, then ask for additional references.

INTERVIEW QUESTIONS

You've found some prospective team members. Now, what do you ask them? Here are some good general questions for everyone you want to add to your team.

1. Who would be a great client for you?
2. Who would be a bad client for you?

Listen to their answers. Are you okay with those parameters? Can you be a good client for them?

Ask the tough questions right up front. If cost is your number-one consideration, say so and ask their price. If response time is the most important thing (and you'll generally pay more for top-notch responsiveness), ask what the rules in the organization are. If resourcefulness is most important, ask them for examples of how they have added to the value of a transaction or property for a client. Do you consider that resourceful?

One comment on price—you do get what you pay for. If price is a big consideration, you might take a look at the deal. Why can't you afford the best?

Following are some of the specific interview questions that we recommend for certain specialities:

Top Five Questions for Real Estate Agents

1. Do you invest in real estate?
2. How can you spot a "good deal"?
3. What do you recommend I do to get top price when I'm selling my home?
4. What are cost efficient ways to add value to my property?
5. In this market, what can we expect for pre-tax and after-tax returns?

Top Five Questions for Property Managers

1. How much real estate do you personally own?
2. What process do you go through before taking on a tenant?
3. How and where do you find new tenants?
4. What could I do to increase the rents on my property?
5. What's the total occupancy of your managed portfolio?

Top Five Questions for a CPA

1. Do you invest in real estate?
2. How many of your clients invest in real estate?
3. What tax incentives are available for real estate investors?
4. What can I do to get the maximum tax benefit from the real estate I currently own?
5. How can I create tax credits in addition to tax deductions?

Top Five Questions for Attorneys

1. What is your speciality?
2. Do you invest in real estate?
3. How many of your clients invest in real estate?
4. What are the most important things for me to do to protect myself during a transaction?
5. Who would be your favorite type of client?

ACTION STEPS

1. What is the one most compelling thing you must know from each team member you add to your team? (Examples might be cost, experience, responsiveness, education.)

   _____

2. What is one action step you can take right now to take your team to another level?

   _____

   I commit to performing the above action steps by _____
   (date).

   Signature:_____

   Today's Date: _____

Chapter 14

BUILDING A TEAM THAT WORKS

NOW IS THE TIME TO BUILD

If you have properly interviewed your team members, it's now time to begin building a true team with them. Trust them. Ask powerful questions. Listen. This is more than just hiring a person that you call up with demands or questions occasionally. The stronger your relationship is with informed, experienced advisors, the better your results will be.

TRUST

It's been said that people who can't trust others really can't trust themselves. Well, whatever the reason is, the quickest way

The Insider's Speed Method for Turning Bad Questions into Good Questions

He said: "Can I write off my car?"
She said: "No."

(Bad Question, Accurate Answer)

He said: "How can I write off my car?"
She said: "It would have to be owned by a company."
He said: "How would I get a company to own my car?"
She said: "First, you would need to have a company with a legitimate business purpose. Then, you would also have to use the car in that business. Your company will need to own the car. One method of transferring your car into the business would be to sell your car to your company at the fair market value."

(Good Questions, Accurate Answers)

to turn off a qualified advisor is to not trust him. Neither Dolf nor Diane need the money they make from their books, seminars, or other businesses. Both are completely financially independent based solely on their real estate investments. Why do we write books and speak publicly, holding ourselves out for public scrutiny? It's because we are passionate about the education we provide and the transformations we are privileged to be part of when a person realizes the truth about real estate investing and tax loopholes. If you can find people to be part of your team who are passionate about the work they perform and the information they give, cherish them. Trust them. Their only ulterior motive is your success.

POWERFUL QUESTIONS

The way you ask the question can greatly affect the answer. For example, if you ask an accountant, "Can I write off my car?" the answer will generally be an easy "No." But if instead you ask, "How can I write off my car?" he must create a solution. You'll get better answers from questions that cause the other person to think about a response. Lousy answers are the result of lousy questions. Great answers come from great questions.

BUILDING A TEAM

Many people feel that if they search long and hard enough they will find the very best bookkeeper, property manager, and so on out there and that once they've found that person, everyone lives happily ever after. In reality, no one person in a particular field is likely to have all of the answers. It sometimes pays to have several professionals in one field on your team. They needn't even be in competition. It could be, for example, that you have one attorney who deals with commercial real estate contracts and another one who handles residential contracts.

Sometimes a little competition is healthy. For instance, we

think it is not very smart to put all your properties with one management company. If one company manages your entire real estate portfolio (and those of other clients as well), then if you have a vacancy, why would the manager fill your property as opposed to any other client's? Now consider engaging two or more property managers where each has full knowledge of the other's existence. They know that in all probability you're going to acquire even more real estate, and that when you do, you're going to have to choose between having this extra property managed by them or by the competition. Now they have a huge incentive to fill your vacant property (over that of any other client with a vacancy) because doing so could sway you to give them your new acquisition to manage.

LISTEN

It's your responsibility to find good team members, discuss your plan, and answer their requests for information. Then, the most valuable habit you can form is to simply listen to their advice. Here are some of the things we were recently told by highly qualified advisors who all have personal experience in their own real estate investing.

Elaine Harshbarger, a real estate agent, has been investing in real estate personally for over five years. Her advice for the first-time real estate investor is to simply "relax." She's recounted the story of a property closing where a brand-new investor had an actual panic attack as she started to sign the papers. Although the investor owned her own home prior to this, buying an investment property brought up all the feelings of loss. What if it didn't work? What if she not only lost this property but her own home as well? Elaine's advice is to do your homework up front, know what you want, and then trust your advisors. By the way, the novice real estate investor did great with her first real estate property. She went on to buy more properties and never had a panic attack again.

Sherri Cossman, an escrow officer with Security Title Company, has over 30 years of experience in the real estate business and almost as many as a real estate investor. She is a wealth of information! One of her pieces of advice to new real estate investors is to really understand the transactional process of transferring title. It's a lot of paperwork and can take longer than you expect. Often the closing date is really just a target date. Yet this legal system we have provides the basis for our strong real estate market. Her advice for success is to purchase the right property, work with professionals, have clear and written objectives of what you want, get good marketable title, and reduce risk wherever you can.

Alec Tanner of Morgan Capital of Arizona has been a mortgage broker for 12 years and a real estate investor for 9 years. In that time, he's accumulated 30 properties. Alec started his career when he moved down from South Dakota with $300, his car, and all the clothes he could fit in it. He moved into a rented room and went to the Salvation Army to buy a frying pan, a can opener, and a spoon. Now, 12 years later, he lives in a multimillion-dollar mansion and has a lucrative portfolio. How? He did it all through real estate. Alec's advice is to really understand loans and to include your mortgage broker in your initial plans. In fact, he suggests you show them your business plan. A good broker will have over 200 options for loans. The more she knows about you, the better the advice she will give you.

Alec also feels that education about loans is critical. And, true to form, he has some great information to share about the entire loan process.

A common type of loan for the real estate investor or business owner is a "stated income" loan. This type of loan does not require income verification. Lenders consider the lack of verifiable income to be added risk. The lender will calculate a qualifying debt ratio based on the income that the borrower states on the application. Verification of the source of income is required. Not all stated income loans are eligible to wage earners. Many lenders want stated income borrowers to be self-employed for two years and provide a letter from their CPA confirming this.You can be self-employed simply by filing a Schedule C for two consecutive years. The Schedule C does not need to show income.

Another tip that Alec gives is if you currently own a primary residence when you decide to pursue investing in real estate, any equity you may have in that property is a potential source of down payment for future properties. If you will be refinancing or getting a home equity line of credit, you should arrange this well in advance. If you ultimately opt to lease out your current residence and purchase a new primary, remember that you will be able to tap into more equity on your existing property while it is owner occupied. A lender cannot give you loans on two primary residences at one time. A lender will not give you an owner-occupied loan on a new primary residence that is less expensive than your current one.

Finally, Alec also gives great advice regarding your credit rating. If you are tapping equity in an existing property to purchase subsequent properties, this is a good time to examine your credit history. In a stated income transaction, good credit is crucial. Ask your loan officer what you can do to improve your credit rating. Paying down revolving debt is often very effective in improving a credit score. Remember that if you are getting a home equity line of credit on an existing property, that this is a revolving debt. When you max out this credit line, it may lower your credit rating.

These little snippets from conversations with qualified advisors/investors show how valuable simply listening to your team can be. To quote Alec, "After all, you're not doing all this just to buy real estate. You're buying real estate to make money." Anyone can buy real estate. It takes skill to make money doing it.

ACTION STEPS

What action step can you take to build a team that brings deals to you and provides necessary education?

_____

_____

I commit to performing the above action steps by _____
(date).

Signature:_____

Today's Date: _____

Appendix A

FREQUENTLY ASKED QUESTIONS

1. *How can I find a property that has a positive* ___ *flow in a strong appreciation area such as Southern C.___ ___ia?*

   In general, prices are a result of appreciati___ ___ rent is a result of inflation. If you're looking for proper___ ___ area that has a higher rate of appreciation than inf___ ___ you will have to do some creative thinking in order to i___ ___sh-flowing property. That's because the rents have not ___ ___p with the appreciation rate.

   Some possible solutions:

   ■ Look for properties with problems. One of Diane's clients is a very successful real estate broker in San Francisco. He always finds properties with great cash flow in a high appreciation area with rent control. His secret is to look for a property that has at least two problems that he knows he can solve. For example, a property that he bought had a bad foundation, needed earthquake reengineering, and had tenants who were grandfathered in with rent control. In other words, there was a lot of tough work to do, and the current tenants would pay the still very low rent when it was all done. There weren't many takers and so he was able to buy it for a low price.

He solved all those problems using the best in legal advisors, architects, and contractors. When he was done, he ended up with a very valuable building with condominiums that he was able to sell for a great profit.

- Use the "Rent to Own" program as your exit strategy to improve cash flow. Buy a single-family unit for the best price you can and then price it based on a sale two or three years out based on current appreciation. In other words, if the property is currently valued at $500,000 and appreciation has been 15 percent per year, you would be looking at a value of $661,250 in two years. You might even make a great deal for your tenant buyer and give them credit for 30 percent of that appreciation . . . or roughly $50,000.

  In other words, your buyer will exercise an option (or buy the property) for $580,000 in two years when the value is estimated to be $661,250! The monthly payments you have received would be based on the amount of the future purchase price, so it is much higher than regular rent. This is a quick two-paragraph report on how a Rent to Own program might work. For a complete article *for free* go to www.DolfAndDiane.com and register for the Insider's Guide Reading Club.

- Also see the insider tips in Chapter 2 on how to translate appreciation into cash flow.

2. *What do you think about buying pre-foreclosures or foreclosures, buying at tax sales, or any of the other ideas promoted on late-night television?*

The methods you talked about—pre-foreclosure, foreclosure, tax sales, and the like—are all valid ways to buy real estate. In fact, we believe that all education is good. The secret is to ask yourself what you are going to do with that information. Are you ready to move forward with investing? Instead of looking for that one more piece of "how do I do this . . . ," may we suggest that you *today* begin building your team and with the help of strong, reliable team members take the first step toward building your financial freedom through real estate?

3. *Should I buy just for cash flow if there is limited appreciation?*

In some parts of the country, the real estate has hit bottom and stayed there. Yet, the basic need for housing continues. In these areas cash-flowing property is very easy to come by, but the areas don't appreciate much.

One of Diane's clients lived in Manhattan, but found investing tough in that market. Yet, he was able to retire from Manhattan to Arizona after just five years of investing in real estate. How did he do it? He bought for cash flow in western/upstate New York, primarily in the Buffalo area. Buffalo had seen a decline in house prices to a point where it just didn't seem like prices could go much lower. Chris Szabo discovered that while the prices plummeted to as low as $35,000 for a house, there was still a big market for renters. In fact, he advertised an open house for one of his rental properties. He had bought the house for $35,000 and was asking $650 per month in rent. The open house was scheduled for 1 to 5 P.M. on a Sunday afternoon. Chris pulled up in front of the house at 12:30 P.M. to discover over 30 people in line. In fact, an ice cream vendor had set up shop in front of his house to sell ice cream. He rented the property easily that first day.

Yet, Buffalo still has an appreciation rate lower than the national appreciation rate. It's that low appreciation rate that makes it such an attractive market for cash-flowing property.

Is that the right plan for you? The answer depends on what you want. Chris and his wife Joanne wanted passive income so that they could start a family without the pressure of work for either of them. In less than five years of investing in the Buffalo area (now expanded to Arizona), they achieved that!

4. *Does it make sense to pay off my house?*

The only way that it makes sense is if you really need to pay off the house to sleep at night and are tired of making money. A house mortgage provides low-cost money for investing plus protects the equity in your home.

Here's how it works. If you borrow against your home, it is often the cheapest money you can find for other investments. The money that you pay 6 percent or 7 percent interest for might make you 20 percent or more. Of course, if you don't have a good use for the money, don't borrow it!

Debt also protects the equity in the house. You see, if you have a lot of equity in your house, it might be wide open to a lawsuit. One little mistake—an accident, someone trips at your house or your child does something—and you might lose your house. But, if you have a large mortgage recorded against the house, it will be much less of a target for an attorney.

5. *I can't make the property cash flow as it is; should I pay off the loan?*

If you've invested in the property in order to provide cash flow, then you've got a problem. What can you do to create the cash flow that is needed? If you're in a highly appreciating area where it is hard to create cash-flowing properties, review the sections in this book that give strategies to create additional income.

If all else fails, maybe this isn't a good property to continue to own. Generally, we recommend that you don't sell properties, but this might be that one exception to the rule.

6. *How can I protect my property from lawsuits?*

There are definitely risks associated with owning property. We call them tenants! Besides the normal risk that comes with owning assets in a litigious country, there is also risk associated with what you might accidentally do. You need to protect your property!

There are three basic ways to protect your property:

a. Adequate insurance.
b. Debt (to reduce equity).
c. Proper business structure.

Additionally, if you have a home, you can take advantage of the homestead exemption. The amount of homestead exemption, which is the amount of equity protected by law, varies by state.

7. *How can I find a good accountant where I live?*

A speaker at a recent AICPA (American Institute of Certified Public Accountants) convention said that, in his opinion, 80 percent of accountants do not understand the basic accounting and tax law for real estate. If you're serious about real estate investing, you'll need to find the

20 percent of CPAs that understand real estate transactions. And if you want to be a *creative* real estate investor, you'll need to find the top 2 percent of CPAs. It's quite possible that there won't be a good accountant who understands real estate in your area. If there isn't, you have a few options: (1) move, (2) settle for a less skilled accountant, or (3) find a qualified CPA in another area that has a systemized approach to working with clients in other states.

8. *How can I find property when I don't have enough time?*

There are three things you have that you can use to invest with: (1) your time, (2) your money, and (3) your talent. Of these, your time is the least leverageable item and it's also the scarcest resource. Your talent will give you the most value. If you have a special negotiation skill or maybe a knack for spotting possibilities of what could be, you can use that talent to make a lot of money. Look at all of the steps involved in actually investing in real estate. What are you good at and what are you not good at?

One of the most time-consuming things you could do would be weeding through hundreds, perhaps thousands, of properties to find that one investment that is right for you. The easiest solution is to hire a real estate agent who, under your specific guidance, can find properties for you to review.

Dolf also didn't have a lot of time in 2003. But, he had a great system and partner so that he was able to buy 52 houses in 36 weeks. If he can do it, *anyone* can do it!

9. *Is there a real estate bubble? What if the value of property in my area goes down?*

All we can say is we sure hope there is a real estate bubble. Too many novice buyers have flooded the real estate market, buying everything in sight without good analysis. This has driven the prices up in the market and has also created a huge opportunity for the sophisticated buyer who is willing to wait for a downturn. Meanwhile, learn about real estate investing. Practice on some properties so that when the opportunity is there, you'll be ready to act.

10. *How do I transfer my property into an LLC (or other protected entity)?*

One of the concerns about real estate investing is how you can protect the property from lawsuits. If you're holding a property for long term, the LLC business structure makes sense in most states.

Once you're sure that the LLC is the right business structure, how do you transfer your property into this entity? If you haven't bought the property yet, buy it in the LLC's name. In some cases, the mortgage company won't allow you to do this. So, you're faced with how to transfer it after the fact.

Or, you might already have purchased property in your own name and now discover that you need to transfer into the LLC.

The problem is the ambiguous wording in most loans. There is usually a due-on-sale clause. This clause means that the entire loan balance is due if you transfer title. Avoid triggering the due-on-sale clause.

First, check with your lender to see if they will allow you to make the transfer. If you get someone who isn't very clear on what it is you want to do, ask to speak to someone with more authority. (If someone doesn't understand, the answer will likely be "no.") If that doesn't work (and we find that it does indeed work over half of the time), you have four alternatives:

a. Do not transfer at all.
b. Transfer the name anyway by just changing the title.
c. Do not transfer, and do an unrecorded sale.
d. Transfer ownership through a land trust.

Of these, options (c) and (d) are the most preferable.

11. *How do I get started? I don't have a lot of money.*

There are three things you can exchange: time, money, and talent. If you don't have money, use your time and talent.

One of Diane's employees at DKA is a single mom who is raising her teenage son with no support or outside help. She barely was able to keep up with her current expenses. There definitely wasn't any additional money left over for investments. But, she was a highly trained bookkeeper who understood real estate. She traded her time and training as a bookkeeper for a part ownership in a real estate transaction.

12. *I currently invest in single-family residences; how do I move to the commercial market?*

The commercial real estate market is indeed different— the numbers are bigger. In general, though, the same principles of analysis and education first are applicable. We strongly recommend that you also assess your team to make sure they have the skills you need to invest at the commercial or multifamily level.

13. *There are so many different ways to make money in real estate—foreclosure, pre-foreclosure, flips, and just plain rentals. What should I do?*

All of these real estate investing techniques and markets

work. What is best for you? It depends on what your desired outcome is and what you have available to invest.

If you need money, it might make sense to do a couple of flips first to create the cash you need to invest in other deals. If you have plenty of income and are looking for write-offs and you or your spouse can qualify as a real estate professional, you might be more interested in a long-term rental property.

Real estate really is just a product. Think about having a lemon. The lemon can be used to make lemonade, lemon juice, seasonings, or even furniture polish. These are all derivatives of the original product. Real estate is like that—you can make money flipping properties, holding them long term, rehabbing property, or even making loans to others who want to invest in real estate. What's the best plan? It completely depends on what you want and what your current Investor IQ is.

14. *How can I get my other questions answered?*

We want your questions! Go to www.DolfAndDiane.com. We give you four different ways that you can get your questions answered.

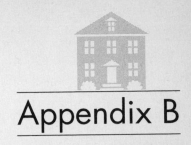

Appendix B

SHORT VERSION OF THIS BOOK

This short version is designed for people who want to go back to their job and claim that they read a terrific real estate investing book during their lunch hour. Of course, if your plan is to actually quit that job at some point because you have been so successful at real estate, you'll want to come back later and actually read this book. And, if you really want to be successful, you'll also complete the action steps at the end of each chapter.

VALID REASONS WHY YOU CAN'T INVEST IN REAL ESTATE

Oh, come on, you've heard these! These are all the reasons why everyone you know doesn't even want to read this book. The most common, without a doubt is:

There are no good deals left.

Have you ever noticed than when you have a theory, you will always find evidence to support it? People who truly believe that there are no good deals left will have their theories validated. If you believe strongly enough that there are no good deals, you will have to settle for lousy deals.

These days, more than ever before, people are mobile. We move because of new jobs, new families, divorce, marriage, death, and just general changes in our life. In fact, the average American moves every five to six years. This means that more than 12 million homes are bought and sold every year. Many of these will be great deals.

Now, here is the best news of all—you don't need to find the good deals yourself. There is an army of diligent, hard-working professionals who are already finding great deals. We call them real estate agents.

FIVE FUNDAMENTAL WEALTH-BUILDING CONCEPTS OF REAL ESTATE

Any fool with money can buy real estate. It's not buying real estate that is the goal. It's using real estate to achieve the goals you've set for yourself. You can maximize the unique wealth-building concepts of real estate to gain even further benefit.

These wealth-building concepts are:

1. Leverage of money.
2. Leverage of time.
3. Velocity.
4. Cash flow.
5. Risk reduction.

Do you want to know more about how to take advantage of these concepts? You'll need to explore Chapter 4! One warning, though; if you've read this and are sure that leverage of money means more debt (and that is sort of the right answer), we'll give you some financial planning for real estate investor tidbits first. In fact, if you've ever used your credit card because of an emergency such as your car breaking down or an unforeseen medical expense or even a sudden urge for a new purse or car, you'll learn how you can still have those things, but never have to use your credit card. That's all in Chapter 4 as well.

WHAT'S YOUR INVESTOR IQ?

Chances are you picked up this book because you want to either begin investing or take your current investing up a notch. Take the test in Chapter 5 to determine where you are now and what you can do about it.

I WANT TO BE RICH, I DON'T HAVE MONEY, AND MY CREDIT STINKS!

Now we're down to the real issues. How can you find money when you don't have any? How can you find credit when the bank says no? And, although this isn't immediately asked, how can you evaluate a property? And, once purchased, what are things you can do for a little money that give you a huge increase in value?

Of course, we answer all of those questions in *The Insider's Guide to Making Money in Real Estate*. But, there is another important question to consider here first for the person who has bad credit and no money. *Why?* What is it about this person's past actions that has created this problem and what action steps should be done first to stop a former financial pattern from repeating? The most important chapter to read in this case might very well be Chapter 3, "What It Really Takes to Succeed in Real Estate." It's not a case of simply tapping into all the people anxious to give you money, although they really do exist. It's a case of first understanding what has caused the current situation.

CYCLES OF A PROPERTY

On this whirlwind tour, we've covered just a few of the topics related to real estate investing. Now, how do you put it together? If you're the kind of person who likes step-by-step guidance through the process (and by the way, the authors both love systems), then you'll enjoy reviewing the steps of a property cycle:

Take It Down

There are actually six steps to the take-it-down cycle:

1. Find it.
2. Evaluate it.

3. Lock it up.
4. Due diligence.
5. Final decision.
6. Buy it.

Stabilize It

Remember the concepts of value engineering if you do rehab work. Make every penny count not just once, but many times over. Basically, you want a stable "turnkey" property. It generally takes up to six months to stabilize a property. The bigger the property, the longer the time needed to settle it out.

Put It On the Shelf

You've bought your property and you've stabilized it. Now, enjoy the fruits of your labor and wait. We recommend that you determine critical points for your property so that you can actually step back from worrying about daily analysis of the property. Some of the critical points you might establish are:

- Gross rent collected.
- Vacancy rate.
- Repair costs.
- Utility costs.
- Minimum cash flow.
- Equity buildup.

The goal is to determine when is the time to refinance, when is the time to review the current property management, and when is the time to exit the property.

BUILDING A TEAM YOU CAN TRUST

You can invest strictly as a do-it-yourselfer, but you will soon run into the one limitation every single one of us has—time. Have you ever listened to how many people lament, "If I only had more time!" You can create more time by building a team that supports your goals.

How do you find that time? First of all, determine who you need and then ask a few powerful questions. In fact, we can generally make a decision within 10 minutes of meeting any potential new advisor. Five critical questions are contained in Chapter 12.

The advisors you choose will help you, or harm you, on your path. Choose wisely.

You had a lot of choices when it came to picking up a real estate book. Thanks for investing the few minutes it took to read this short version. Now, go back and read it the old-fashioned way and do the *action steps* along the way. Use the resources we've provided throughout the book. Both authors are experienced investors, and we've both made some mistakes along the way with our investing. Learn from those mistakes, so you don't need to repeat them! And, equally, learn from the things that worked, so you can repeat and even exceed the good results we experienced.

Wealth is a pathway—enjoy your journey. Happy investing!

Meet Dolf de Roos

Dr. Dolf de Roos began investing in real estate as an undergraduate student. Despite going on to earn a Ph.D. in electrical and electronic engineering from the University of Canterbury, Dolf increasingly focused on his flair for real estate investing, which has enabled him to have never had a job. He has, however, invested in many classes of real estate (residential, commercial, industrial, hospitality, and specialist) all over the world.

Today he is the chairman of the public company Property Ventures Limited, an innovative real estate investment company whose stated mission is to massively increase stockholders' worth. Over the years, Dolf was cajoled into sharing his investment strategies, and he has run seminars on the Psychology of Creating Wealth and on Real Estate Investing throughout North America, Australia, New Zealand, Asia, the Middle East, and Europe since the 1980s.

Beyond sharing his investment philosophy and strategies with tens of thousands of investors (beginners as well as seasoned experts), Dolf has also trained real estate agents, written and published numerous bestselling books on property (including *The New York Times* best seller *Real Estate Riches*) and introduced computer software designed to analyze and manage properties quickly and efficiently. He often speaks at investors' conferences, real estate agents' conventions, and his own international seminars, and regularly takes part in radio shows and television debates. Born in New Zealand, raised in Australia, New Zealand, and Europe, Dolf, with six languages up his sleeve, offers a truly global perspective on the surprisingly lucrative wealth-building opportunities of real estate.

To find out what you can learn from Dolf's willingness to share his knowledge about creating wealth through real estate, and to receive his free monthly newsletter, please visit his web site www.dolfderoos.com.

Meet Diane Kennedy

Diane Kennedy, the nation's preeminent tax strategist, is owner of D Kennedy & Associates, a leading tax strategy and accounting firm, and the author of *The Wall Street Journal* and *BusinessWeek* best sellers, *Loopholes of the Rich* and *Real Estate Loopholes*.

Diane's extensive teachings have empowered people throughout the country to minimize their tax liabilities through the use of legal tax loopholes.

Diane has written for *The Tax Savings Report, Investment Advisor Magazine, Personal Excellence*, the Money & Finance section of *Balance* magazine, and *Healthy Wealthy n Wise*, where she has a regular column. She's been featured in *Kiplinger's Personal Finance, The Wall Street Journal, USA Today*, and the *Associated Press* and on *CNN, CNNfn, Bloomberg TV* and *Radio, CNBC, StockTalkAmerica*, and numerous regional TV and radio shows.

A highly sought-after international speaker and educator, she has dedicated her career to empowering and educating others about financial investments and the tax advantages that are available. Through Diane's knowledge and execution of legal tax loopholes in her business and real estate investments, she and her husband Richard are able to contribute to special life-changing projects and charities in the United States and third-world countries.

Diane provides critical tax law updates, advice on the latest tax loopholes, as well as tax-advantaged wealth building resources on her web site: www.TaxLoopholes.com (821 North Fifth Avenue, Phoenix, AZ 85003, 1-888-592-4769).

Index

Accountability, 66

Accountant, *see* Certified Public Accountant (CPA)
functions of, 55, 197, 204
recruitment sources, 220–221

Active appreciation:
benefits of, 38, 155
commercial properties, 42–43
examples of, 41–42
multifamily properties, 42–43
residential properties, 42
tenant needs, 43–44
value appraisal, 154

Active management, 53

Advisors, *see specific types of advisors*
functions of, 94
recruitment sources, 202–204
selection factors, 84

Age factor, 16, 28–29

Air-conditioning systems, 48–49

Air space, 123–124

Alarm system, 21, 42

American Institute of Certified Public Accountants (AICPA), 220

Americans with Disabilities Act (ADA), retrofitting costs, 56–57

Amortization, 55

Analysis, importance of, 19

Appearance of property, 41–42, 163

Appreciation, *see specific types of appreciation*
active, 38, 41–44, 154–155
capital, 25
defined, 55
neighborhood, 40–41
passive, 38–41, 39, 155
potential for, 19

Area trends, 19

Asking price, 151

Asset protection, 22, 90–94, 220

Assets, secured debt and, 22

Attorney:
functions of, 197, 204
interview questions for, 206

Audiotapes, 53

Automobile, tax deductions, 53–54

Average appreciation, value appraisal, 153

Background checks, 194

Bad credit, 17, 29, 228–229

Bad debt, 95

Bank, as lender, 23, 34–36

Belief system, significance of, 65–69

Blue-chip stocks, 34

The Secret to Making Money in Real Estate

Visit www.DolfAndDiane.com for innovative real estate investment strategies that increase cash flow and build wealth.

By registering as a DolfAndDiane Reader, you'll be able to access hundreds of ideas and resources that support you in your real estate endeavors. Make more money and pay less tax!

- **FREE Access to Vital Statistics for Your Real Estate Investments**

    What is the average appreciation in your area? Where is the highest national appreciation? Learn all this and more at www.DolfAndDiane.com.

- **FREE Tips to Increase Your Wealth Velocity**

    How fast does your wealth grow? Are you ready to learn more information on how to make it grow even faster?

- **Take a Peek at Dolf's and Diane's Rolodex—filled with resources to maximize your real estate investments. FREE resource guide!**

- **FREE eBook Financial Planning for Real Estate Investors**

This is information you can't find any place else. And, it's free just for signing up as a DolfAndDiane Reader at www.DolfAndDiane.com.

Dear Friends,

We are not just two authors who want to sell you another book about real estate investing. We want to be your coaches in your real estate adventure! Get started by signing up as a DolfAndDiane Reader. You'll receive hundreds of ideas and resources to help you make more money from your real estate today for FREE.

Please join us and other like-minded people in sharing knowledge that increases wealth. Together, we make a difference.

Successful Investing,

Diane Kennedy   Dolf de Roos